THE POET'S CRAFT

Poetry is not like reasoning, a power to be exerted according to the determination of the will. A man cannot say, 'I will compose poetry'. SHELLEY

That talk of inspiration is sheer nonsense; there is no such thing. It is a mere matter of craftsmanship.
WILLIAM MORRIS

Deux sortes de vers: les vers donnés et les vers calculés.
PAUL VALÉRY

ALSO BY A. F. SCOTT

FROM PARAGRAPH TO ESSAY I & II
A YEAR'S WORK IN PRÉCIS
ENGLISH COMPOSITION, BOOKS I–IV
POEMS FOR PLEASURE, BOOKS I–III
(Cambridge University Press)

MEANING AND STYLE
POETRY AND APPRECIATION
MODERN ESSAYS, 1939–41
MODERN ESSAYS, 1941–43
MODERN ESSAYS, 1943–51
COUNTRY LIFE
TOPICS AND OPINIONS
(Macmillan & Co.)

THE POET'S CRAFT

A COURSE IN THE
CRITICAL APPRECIATION OF POETRY

based on the study of holograph manuscripts,
earlier and later versions of printed poems,
transpositions of prose into verse,
and contrasted translations

BY

A. F. SCOTT

WITH A SELECTION OF
UNSIGNED POEMS AND PASSAGES
FOR APPRECIATION

CAMBRIDGE
AT THE UNIVERSITY PRESS
1957

PUBLISHED BY
THE SYNDICS OF THE CAMBRIDGE UNIVERSITY PRESS

Bentley House, 200 Euston Road, London, N.W. 1
American Branch: 32 East 57th Street, New York 22, N.Y.

PUBLISHER'S NOTE

A paper identifying the poems in SECTION V can be
had on application to either of the above addresses.

Printed in Great Britain at the University Press, Cambridge
(Brooke Crutchley, University Printer)

CONTENTS

I. THE POET'S MANUSCRIPT

A selection of photographs and transcriptions
of manuscript poems

CONTENTS

II. THE POET'S PRINTED REVISIONS

A selection of poems and passages of the first edition
compared with a revised, later edition

III. THE POET'S RAW MATERIAL

Material adapted by the poet, presented for
comparison with the poetry

IV. THE POET'S TRANSLATION
Selected translations of the same poems
for comparison

CONTENTS

PREFACE

Browning's Grammarian exclaimed:

> Show me their shaping,
> Theirs, who most studied man, the bard and sage.

This book tries in several different ways to present the 'shaping' of the poets by a close study of their use of language.

The first section consists of reproductions of manuscript poems; Section I many of these are of the original drafts, showing the corrections made as the poem was being composed. A study of these manuscripts gives an insight into the poet's mind and a personal contact not achieved from the printed page alone. We see, as it were, the hand moving across the page expressing thoughts and after-thoughts. We see a word struck out immediately after it was written down and another set in its place, following on at once with a second thought. Sometimes the correction denotes a change of mind; other corrections made above the line or in the margin are obviously not done immediately, but are later additions or substitutions.

It is interesting to note how the work of correction is often quite as inspired as 'the first onrush of words and ideas'. As we examine these manuscript poems we feel with C. M. Bowra that 'the poet must be his own critic and decide which are the right words among the many which come to him; he must exclude much that at first sight looks attractive, and adapt the outpourings of inspiration to the creative impulse which animates his poem'.

To these manuscript poems are added brief notes, and a literal transcription of the text.

The next section presents, for purposes of comparison, the first Section II published version of several well-known poems with the more widely accepted revised version. A brief history of the changes is given so that we may follow some of the poems over a period of years.

SECTION III   The third section deals with the raw material used by the poet. As Sir Henry Newbolt says,

The more a writer struggles to invent the less he is likely to create. His true way is a different one; he finds his material among the accumulated stories of the race, whether ancient or modern; he sets to work to reject all that he judges unnecessary or unfit, to add all that is lacking; and finally, without effort, almost without consciousness of his power, he endows his work with his own personal quality in the act of making it serve his own purpose.

As we consider what Sir Thomas North received from Plutarch, and what Shakespeare received from North we see in action 'a kind of creative evolution'.

SECTION IV   It has been said that the translation of a poem from one language into another is not the making of poetry but its destruction. There have been, however, many fine translations of poetry into English by poets such as Chapman, Dryden, Pope, Cowper, Bridges, and C. Day Lewis. Admittedly, the beauty of their productions depends upon their handling of English, and it is always different from the beauty of the original, because in poetry the meaning of words lies in their sound as much as in their sense.

In the fourth section translations of the same poem (or passage from a long poem) are set down for critical comparison, not as faithful renderings (for that the reader would obviously need an intimate knowledge of the original) but as examples of the poetic style of different poets using the same material. Turning from one poet to another we may appraise such a line as:

> I who queen it through these courts of heaven

against

> I who in high heaven move as a queen

and

> I who through heaven its mistress move

all derived from Virgil's

> Ast ego quae divum incedo regina.

SECTION V   The last section contains a number of unsigned poems arranged according to subject, lending themselves to contrast and comparison.

Included also are some poems given in different versions for close
analysis. Occasionally a poem and the material from which it is
derived gives further opportunity for critical appreciation. Throughout, material is presented for a close analysis of words and language,
leading to a fuller understanding of poetry and the poet's craft.

A. F. SCOTT

27 April 1956

ACKNOWLEDGEMENTS

Section I

The following manuscripts are reproduced by permission of the British Museum:
William Shakespeare: from *Sir Thomas More*; William Cowper: *The Halibut*; William
Wordsworth: from *The Waggoner*; S. T. Coleridge: *Lewti*; P. B. Shelley: from *The
Death of Adonis*; T. L. Beddoes: *Dream Pedlary*; Lord Tennyson: *Milton, Alcaics*;
Robert Browning: from *The Ring and the Book*; E. B. Browning: from *The Runaway
Slave at Pilgrim's Point*; D. G. Rossetti: *Love's Compass*; Christina Rossetti: *Sleeping at
Last*; A. C. Swinburne: from *Rococo*.

George Herbert: *Perfection* is reproduced by permission of Dr Williams's Library;
John Milton: from *Lycidas* by permission of Trinity College Library, Cambridge;
Thomas Gray: from *Elegy written in a Country Churchyard* by permission of Eton
College Library; George Crabbe: *Jane Adair* by permission of the University Library,
Cambridge; William Blake: *The Tyger* by permission of Mrs William Emerson; Lord
Byron: *Oh! snatch'd away in Beauty's Bloom* by permission of Sir John Murray; John
Keats: from *Ode to the Nightingale* by permission of the Syndics of the Fitzwilliam
Museum, Cambridge; G. M. Hopkins: *The Starlight Night* by permission of Mr Gerard
Hopkins, The Society of Jesus and The Bodleian Library, Oxford; Edward Thomas:
Adlestrop by permission of Mrs Edward Thomas and the British Museum; Rupert
Brooke: the first draft manuscript of *The Soldier* is reproduced by permission of the
author's representatives and of Messrs Sidgwick and Jackson Ltd.; Wilfred Owen:
Anthem for Dead Youth by permission of Messrs Chatto and Windus and the British
Museum; Isaac Rosenberg: from *Moses* by permission of Messrs Chatto and Windus
and the British Museum.

Section IV

F. L. Lucas: Homer, *Odyssey* XXIV, 1–14 is reproduced by permission of the Folio
Society; Thomas Hardy: Catullus, *Ode* XXXI, from *Collected Poems of Thomas Hardy*
(Macmillan) by permission of the publishers and the Trustees of the Hardy Estate;
James Elroy Flecker: Virgil, *Aeneid* VI, 269–294 by permission of Messrs Secker and
Warburg; Robert Bridges: Virgil, *Aeneid* VI, 269–294 from *Ibant Obscuri* (Clarendon Press)
by permission of the publishers; Rolfe Humphries: Virgil, *Aeneid* VI, 269–294 by per-
mission of Messrs Charles Scribner's Sons Ltd.; C. Day Lewis: Virgil, *Georgics* I, 311–
334 by permission of Messrs Jonathan Cape Ltd.; G. S. Fraser: Horace, *Odes* I, v from

ACKNOWLEDGEMENTS

Voices from the Past by James and Janet Maclean Todd (Phoenix House) by permission of the author; H. Rackham: Horace, *Odes* I, ix from *Greece and Rome* (Clarendon Press) by permission of the publishers; A. E. Housman: Horace, *Odes* IV, vii by permission of the Society of Authors as the Literary Representatives of the Trustees of the estate of the late A. E. Housman, and Messrs Jonathan Cape Ltd., publishers of A. E. Housman's *Collected Poems* (and Messrs Henry Holt and Co. Inc., New York); James Maclean Todd: Horace, *Odes* IV, vii from *Voices from the Past* by James and Janet Maclean Todd (Phoenix House) by permission of the author and publishers; Laurence Binyon: Dante, *Paradiso*, Canto XXXIII, 97–145 by permission of the Society of Authors and Mrs Cicely Binyon; Nevill Coghill: Chaucer, *Canterbury Tales, Nonne Preestes Tale*, 1–16 by permission of Penguin Books Ltd.

(In planning this section I found *Voices from the Past* by James and Janet Maclean Todd particularly helpful. A.F.S.)

Section V

Robert Bridges: *Larks* from *The shorter Poems of Robert Bridges* (Clarendon Press) is reproduced by permission of the publishers; W. H. Davies: *Robin Redbreast* from *The Collected Poems of W. H. Davies* (Jonathan Cape) by permission of Mrs H. M. Davies and the publishers; Frank O'Connor: 'A hiding tuft, a greenbarked yewtree' by permission of Messrs A. D. Peters and W. B. Yeats's revised version of the same poem by permission of Mrs W. B. Yeats; Thomas Hardy: *In a Wood* from *Collected Poems of Thomas Hardy* (Macmillan) by permission of the publishers and the Trustees of the Hardy Estate; Sir John Squire: *There was an Indian* by permission of the author; Robert Frost: *Mowing* and *The Line Gang* from *Complete Poems of Robert Frost* (Jonathan Cape) by permission of the publishers; Edward Thomas: *Pewits* and *The Glory* by permission of Mrs Edward Thomas; C. Day Lewis: *Now the full-throated daffodils* from *Collected Poems* 1954 (Hogarth Press) by permission of the publishers; W. B. Yeats: *Her Praise* from *Collected Poems* (Macmillan) by permission of the publishers and of Mrs W. B. Yeats; A. E. Housman: *A Shropshire Lad* XXXI, XLIV and *Last Poems* XXVII by permission of the Society of Authors as the Literary Representative of the Trustees of the estate of the late A. E. Housman, and Messrs Jonathan Cape Ltd., publishers of A. E. Housman's *Collected Poems* (and Messrs Henry Holt and Co. Inc., New York); John Masefield: *On Malvern Hill* by permission of the Society of Authors, Dr John Masefield, O.M., and the Macmillan Company, New York; A. C. Benson: *The Hawk* from *The Poems of Arthur Christopher Benson* (John Lane, the Bodley Head Ltd.) by permission of the publishers; Walter de la Mare: *Song of the Mad Prince* by permission of the Society of Authors as the Literary Representative of the Trustees of the estate of the late Walter de la Mare, and Messrs Faber and Faber Ltd.; Sir A. Quiller-Couch: *Lord, in Thy Courts* from *Poems and Ballads* (Methuen) by permission of Messrs J. M. Dent & Sons; Emily Dickinson: *The Chariot* from *Poems by Emily Dickinson* (Little, Brown and Co., New York); Louis Macneice: *Prognosis* from *Collected Poems* (Faber and Faber Ltd.) by permission of the publishers; Louis Untermeyer: *To a Telegraph Pole* from *Burning Bush* by permission of Harcourt, Brace and Co., New York; G. M. Hopkins: *Inversnaid, Spring* and *The Windhover* from the collected poems of Gerard Manley Hopkins by permission of Oxford University Press.

I

THE POET'S
MANUSCRIPT

MS. Harl. 7368 & 9, British Museum

moo   nay certainly yo^u ar
  for to the king god hath his offyc lent
  of dread of Juſtyce, power and Comaund
  hath bid him rule, and willd yo^u to obay
  and to add ampler ma͞tie to this
he ~~god~~ hath not ~~le~~ only lent the king his figure
    &

  his throne ~~his~~ ſword, but gyven him his owne **name**
  calls him a god on earth, what do yo^u then,
  ryſing gainſt him that god himſealf enſtalls
  but ryſe gainſt god, what do yo^u to yor ſowles
  in doing this o deſperat ~~as~~ as you are.
  waſh your foule mynds w^t teares and thoſe ſame hands
  that yo^u lyke rebells lyft againſt the peace
  lift vp for peace, and your vnreuerent knees
  ~~that~~ make them your feet to kneele to be forgyven
  ~~is ſafer warrs, then euer yo^u can make,~~
      ~~in in to yor obedienc.~~
  ~~whoſe diſcipline is ryot; why even yor warrs hurly~~
  tell me but this
  ~~cannot peeed but by obedienc~~ what rebell captaine
  as muty^nes ar incident, by his name
  can ſtill the rout who will obay ~~th~~ a traytor
  or howe can well that pclamation ſounde
  when their is no adicion but a rebell
  to quallyfy a rebell, youle put downe ſtraingers
  kill them cutt their throts poſſeſſe their howſes
  and leade the ma͞tie of lawe in liom
     ~~alas alas~~
  to ſlipp him lyke a hound; ~~fayeng~~ ſay nowe the king
  as he is clement,. yf thoffendor moorne
  ſhoold ſo much com to ſhort of your great treſpas
   as but to banyſh yo^u, whether woold yo^u go.
  what Country by the nature of yor error
  ſhoold gyve you harber go yo^u to ffraunc or flanders
  to any Jarman pvince, ~~to~~ ſpane or portigall
  nay any where ~~why yo^u~~ that not adheres to Jngland
  why yo^u muſt needs be ſtraingers, woold yo^u be pleaſd
  to find a nation of ſuch barbarous temper
  that breaking out in hiddious violence
  woold not afoord yo^u, an abode on earth
  whett their deteſted knyves againſt yor throtes
  ſpurne yo^u lyke doggs, and lyke as yf that god
  owed not nor made not yo^u, nor that the elaments
      yor
  wer not all appropriat to ~~their~~ Comforts.
  but Charterd vnto them, what woold yo^u thinck
  to be thus vſd, this is the ſtraingers caſe
all   and this your momtaniſh inhumanyty

The H. Scriptures

A servant w'th this clause
Makes drudgery divine:
Who sweepeth a roome, as for thy laws,
Makes that, and th'action fine.

But these are Petti-actions, right & good:
Happy his lott, that & sd light
See thee this light of all these actions
And shew thee him at last thy art.

This is y' famous stone
That turneth all to gold
For y't w'ch God doth touch & owne
Cannot for lesse be told.

The Church.

Perfection. The Elixir.

Lord teach mee to referr
All things I doe to thee
That I not only may not erre
But allso pleasing bee.

A man that looks on glass
On it may stay his eye;
Or if he pleaseth, through it pass
And then the heavn espy.

He that does ought for thee,
Marketh y' deed for thine:
And nowhere his Quick Shaft & Fire,
Thou saist, this fruit is mine.

A Servant of thy parts be
Nothing can be so meane
That & w'th this tincture for thy sake
Will not grow bright & cleane.

The Church

A servant wth this clause,
Makes drudgery divine.
Who sweeps a ~~chamber~~ room, as for thy lawes,
Makes that, and th'action fine.

But these are high perfectns:
Happy are they that dare
Lett in the light to all their actions
And shew them as they are.

This is y^t famous stone
That turneth all to gold
For y^t wch God doth touch & owne
Can not for lefs be told.

The Church
Perfection The Elixir

Lord teach mee to referr
All things I doe to thee
That I not onely may not erre
But allso pleasing bee.

A man that looks on glafs
On it may stay his eye:
Or if he pleaseth through it pafs
And then the heav'en espy

He that does oyght for thee
Marketh y^t deed for thee,
And when the Divell shakes y^t tree
Thou saist, this fruit is mine.

All may of thee pertake:
Nothing can be so ~~low~~, meane
W^{ch} wth his tincture (for thy sake)
grow bright & cleane
Will not ~~~~

5

MS. Trinity College, Cambridge

FROM 'LYCIDAS'

Together both ere the high launs appear'd
under the ~~glimmering~~ *eyelids of the morne   opening*
wee drove afeild, and both together heard
what tyme the gray fly winds her sultrie horne
batning our flocks wth the fresh dews of night
oft till the ~~cah~~ *starre* ~~bright~~ *that rose at Evning bright*
toward heavens defcent had sloop't his ~~burnisht~~ *weele westring*
meane while the rurall ditties were not mute
tempd to th' oaten flute
rough Satyrs danc't; and Fauns wth clov'en heele
from the glad sound would not be absent long
and old Damœtas lov'd to heare our song.
But O the heavie change now thou art ~~gone~~ *gone*
now thou art gon, and never must returne
thee shepheard, thee the woods and desert caves
wth wild Thyme, and the gadding vine oregrowne
and all thire ~~Eegho~~ *Echo's mourne*
the willows, and the hazel copses greene
shall now no more be seene
fanning thire joyous leavs to thy soft lays
as killing as the canker to the rose
*or taint-worme to the weanling heards that graze   *
or frost to flowrs that thire gay ~~blossoms weare weare~~ *wardrope weare*
when first the white thorne blows
such Lycidas thy losse to shepheards eare
Where were yee nymphs when ye remorfelesse deepe
clos'd ore the head of yor ~~your~~ *Lov'd Lycidas*
for neither were yee playing on the steepe
where yor old bards the famous Druids lie
nor on the shaggie top of Mona high
nor yet where Deva spreds her wisard streame
ay mee I fondly dreame
~~had yee~~ *bin there for what could that have don?*
~~what could the golden haird~~ *Calliope*
for her inchaunting son
~~when shee beheld (the gods farr sighted bee)~~
~~his goarie scalpe rowle downe the Thracian lee~~

whome universal nature
might lament
~~and heaven and hel deny~~
when his divine head downe
the streame was sent
downe the swift Hebrus to the
Lefbian shore.

7

MS. Eton College

Oft as the Woodlark piped her farewell Song
With whistful Eyes pursue the setting Sun
                                        spreading   nodding
Oft at the Foot of yonder hoary   Beech
That wreathes its old fantastic Roots so high.
His listlefs Length at Noontide would he stretch,
And pore upon the Brook that babbles by.

   With Gestures quaint now smileing as in Scorn,
        wayward fancies ~~loved~~ *would be*
  Mutt'ring his fond Conceits he ~~wont to~~ *rove:*
     drooping,
  Now woeful wan, ~~he droop'd~~*, as one forlorn*
  Or crazed with Care, or crofs'd in hopelefs Love.

   One Morn we mifs'd him on th' ~~ac~~*customd Hill,*
  Along the   near
  By the Heath- ~~side~~*, & at his fav'rite Tree.*
  Another came, nor yet beside the Rill,
        by
  Nor up the Lawn, nor at the Wood was he.

~~There scatter'd oft, the earliest~~
Then next with Dirges meet in sad Array
    by
Slow thro the Church-way Path we saw him born
Approach & read, for thou can'st read the Lay
  Graved carved   yon
Wrote on the Stone beneath that ancient Thorn
          Year
There scatter'd oft the earliest of y^e ~~Spring~~
      Showers of
By Hands unseen are frequent Vi'lets found
    Redbreast
The Robin loves to build & warble there,
And little Footsteps lightly print the Ground.

Where hast thou floated, in what seas pursued
Thy pastime, when wast thou an egg new-spewed,
Lost in th' immensity of Ocean's waste.
Roar, as they might, the overbearing winds
That rocked the deep, thy cradle, thou wast safe,
And in thy minikin and embryo state,
Attached to the small leaf of some salt weed,
Bidst outlive tempests, that have oft and racked
The joints of many a stout and noble bark
And whelmed them in the unexplored abyss.
Indebted to no magnet and no chart,
Nor under guidance of the polar fire,
Thou wast a voyager on many coasts,
Grazing at large in meadows submarine,
Batavian or Hibernian, at last poised
Where flat Batavia just emerging peeps
Above the brine, where Caledonian rocks shoots
beat back the surge, and where Hibernia spreads
Her causeway far into the deep main
Wherever thou hast fed, thou little thought'st,
And I not more, that I should feed on thee.
Peace therefore and good health and much good fish
Go him who sent thee, and success, as oft
As it descends into the bigbelly gulph
Go the that caught thee. fare thee well,
Thy cot, thy brethren of the fin thou wast doomed
Would envy, could they know that
I feed a bard and to be praised in verse.

MS. Add. 37059 f. 45, British Museum

Where hast thou floated, in what seas purſued
Thy pastime, where wast thou an egg new-spawnd,
Lost in th'immenſity of Oceans waste.
Roar, as they might, the overbearing winds
That rockd the deep, thy cradle, thou wast safe,
And in thy minnikin and embryo state,
       firm
Attachd to the ~~small~~ leaf of some salt weed,
            such as wrung
Didst outlive tempests, ~~that have toſsd~~ and ɪackd
The joints of many a stout and noble ~~fleet~~ bark
     whelmd
And ~~sunk~~ them in the unexplored abyſs
Indebted to no magnet and no chart,
Nor under guidance of the polar fire,
Thou wast a voyager on many coasts,
    Grazing at large ~~many a~~
~~Hast grazed perhaps~~ in meadows submarine,
  _ ~~and~~   und
~~Batavian or Hibernian, or haſt found~~
Where flat Batavia just emerging peeps
    brine   s
Above the ~~wave~~, where Caledoniaɴ rocks
           shoots
Beat back the surge, and where Hibernia ~~spreads~~
  ~~boaſted~~ wondrous
Her cauſeway far into the ~~deep~~ main
Wherever thou hast fed, thou little thoughtst,
  we   we
And ~~I~~ not more, that ~~I~~ should feed on thee
  Peace
~~Have~~ therefore and good health and much good fish
To Him who sent thee, and succeſs, as oft
        billowy
As it deſcends ɪnto the ~~fiſhy~~ gulph
   same drag
To the ~~good boat~~ that caught thee, fare thee well,
    slimey
Thy lot, thy brethren of the ~~nimble~~ fin   doomd
         thou wast
~~Might~~ Would ~~they know~~ envy, could they know that
To feed a bard and to be praised in verſe.

Jane Adair

Wert thou my Love some Vagrant Maid
Who begg'd from Door to Door
...
And good as well as poor
...
I'd lead thee to the Altar Love
And wed with Jane Adair.

Wert thou a Lady of the Land
Thy Charms should be my theme
Still would I ask that lovely hand
Still woo thy fond Esteem
...
To one so good & fair
And do I Deeds I dare not say speak
To wed with Jane Adair.

The Mountains Tops is not so high
But that ... Lowr ...
...
The Treasure that in ... Mountain hid
Adventurous Men explore
Or deep in caverns mine abide
And say the glittering Ore
And shall & melt who toils for gain
more persevering be
Then I who labour to obtain
Love, ... thee my dearest God ...

27| *Jane Adair* |

Wert thou my Love some Vagrant Maid
Who beg'd from Door to Door   ill
                        and   Vice
~~If in the spotless~~ wert thou then of ~~Sin~~ afraid
        true
And good as well as poor
I still wd true & faithful prove   Still   tru. constant|
~~All pride In vain might~~ ~~Then would I still thy prove~~
wd ~~And then J^t with me share~~   To ~~thee mould thy~~
                                 And Fortunes wrongs repair
Id lead thee to the Altar Love
And wed with Jane Adair.

Wert thou a Lady of the Land
Thy Charm s^d be my theme
Still would I ask that lovely hand
Still woo thy fond Esteem
Thro Perils I would win my way
To one so good & fair
And do ∂ Deeds I dare not say speak
To wed with Jane Adair

                              too
The Mountain Top is not so high   mine
But there ∂ Eagles soar the treasures that ∂ ~~Earth~~
                         in   supply
~~The I so deep the as Mines & Treasures lie~~
     Hope
And ~~Yet venturous Men explore~~
The Treasures that in ~~Earth abide~~ Mountains tied
Adventurous Men explore
Or deep in cavernd Mine abide
   And Dig the glittering Ore
And shall ∂ wretch who toils for gain
   More persevering be
Than I who labour to obtain
   Love, Happiness & thee   my dearest Good in thee

Rossetti MS. Mrs Emerson, Boston, Massachusetts

The Tyger

1   Tyger Tyger burning bright
     In the forests of the night
     What immortal hand or eye
~~Dare~~   ~~Could~~ frame thy fearful symmetry

     Burnt in
2   ~~In what~~ distant deeps or skies
~~The cruel~~ ~~Burnt~~ the fire of thine eyes
     On what wings dare he aspire
     What the hand dare sieze the fire

3   And what shoulder & what art
     Could twist the sinews of thy heart
     And when thy heart began to beat
     What dread hand & what dread feet

     ~~Could fetch it from the furnace deep~~
     ~~And in thy horrid ribs dare steep~~
     ~~In the well of sanguine woe~~
     ~~In what clay & in what mould~~
     ~~Were thy eyes of fury rolld~~

     Where   where
4   ~~What~~ the hammer ~~what~~ the chain
     In what furnace was thy brain
                                   dread grasp
     What the anvil what ~~the arm arm grasp clasp~~
~~Dare~~   ~~Could~~ its deadly terrors ~~clasp grasp~~ clasp

6   Tyger Tyger burning bright
     In the forests of the night
     What immortal hand & eye
          frame
     Dare ~~form~~ thy fearful symmetry

Rossetti MS. Mrs Emerson, Boston, Massachusetts

Burnt in distant deeps or skies
The cruel fire of thine eye,
Could heart descend or wings aspire
What the hand dare seze the fire

         dare he ~~smile laugh~~
5 ~~3~~ And ~~did he laugh~~ his work to see
         ankle
~~What the shoulder what the knee~~
Dare
4 ~~Did~~ he who made the lamb make thee
1 When the stars threw down their spears
2 And waterd heaven with their tears

Tyger Tyger burning bright
In the forests of the night
What Immortal hand & eye
Dare frame thy fearful symmetry

And what shoulder & what art
Could twist the sinews of thy heart
And when thy heart began to beat
What dread hand & what dread feet

When the stars threw down their spears
And waterd heaven with their tears
Did he smile his work to see
Did he who made the lamb make thee

Tyger Tyger burning bright
In the forests of the night
What immortal hand & eye
Dare frame thy fearful symmetry

MS. Ashley 4637, British Museum

world
Commingling with the scene that lies
In peace before their outward eyes
Rocks clouds and stars a solemn
                  show
Repeated in the lake below
A prospect in itself serene
Brave world for Poet's eye to see
~~*But*~~ *But restless to their heaven*
O fancy what a jubilee   *a scene*
Pregnant with rare imagination
           multiplied
Rich change of manifold creation

Of colour bright as feverish dreams,
Commingling as they come and go
With clouds, rocks, stars, majestic show
Repeated in the lake below
  The heav'ns the air the abyſs serene
A prospect ~~in itself serene~~
  Of waters all a restleſs scene
But ~~restleſs to their eyes a scene~~
Pregnant with rare Imagination
Rich change and multiplied creation
Brave world for Poet's eye to see
O Fancy what a Jubilee
This sight
  Both   *abyſs*
The heaven above the ~~deep~~ serene
Of ~~waters,~~
~~A restleſs undivided scene~~
  An ab spangled
  An undivided restleſs scene
  The heavens above, th'abyſs serene
  Fill'd with my restleſs ſpirit, a scene
  Pregnant with rare Imagination.
Commingling as they come and go
With rocks clouds stars, majestic show
Repeated in the lake below,
  Earth   *Brave world &*
  Air spangled sky and lake serene
~~The spangled heavens, the abyſs serene~~
  Involv'd and restleſs all — a scene
~~Of waters and the air between~~
~~Involved and restleſs all — a scene~~
Pregnant with rare imagination
Rich change and multiplied creation
Air, spangled sky and lake serene
Involved and restleſs all — a scene

spangled
starry, above the abyſs serene
The heavens the air, that
The element all between
~~An~~ involved and restleſs scene *all, a scene*
The heavens the abyſs serene

The ~~Circassian~~ Circassian's Love-chaunt.

High o'er the ~~rocks~~ rocks at night I rov'd 2.
To forget the form, I lov'd.
Image of ~~mine~~ Lewti! from my mind
Depart! for ~~mine~~ Lewti is not kind!

Bright was the Moon: the Moon's bright beam
Speckled with many a moving shade,
Danc'd upon Tamaha's stream;
But brightlier on the Rock it play'd,
The Rock, half-shelter'd from my view
By pendent boughs of tressy Yew!
True to Love, but false to Rest,
My fancy whisper'd in my breast—
So shines my ~~mine~~ Lewti's forehead fair
Gleaming thro' her sable hair.
Image of ~~mine~~ Lewti! from my mind
Depart! for ~~mine~~ Lewti is not kind..

I saw a cloud of whitest hue;
Onward to the Moon it pass'd!
Still brighter and more bright it grew
With floating colours not a few,
Till it reach'd the moon at last

MS. Add. 35343, British Museum

The ~~Wild Indian's~~ Love-chaunt.
Circaſsian's

         rocks
High o'er the ~~silver~~ at night I rov'd
To forget the form, I lov'd.
         Lewti!
Image of ~~Cora~~ from my mind
         Lewti
Depart! for ~~Cora~~ is not kind!

Bright was the Moon: the Moon's bright beam
Speckled with many a moving Shade,
Danc'd upon Tamaha's stream;
But brightlier on the Rock it play'd,
The Rock, half-shelter'd from my view
By pendent boughs of treſsy Yew!
True to Love, but false to Rest,
My fancy whisper'd in my breast —
         Lewti's
So shines my ~~Cora's~~ forehead fair
Gleaming thro' her sable hair.
         Lewti
Image of ~~Cora!~~ from my mind
         Lewti
Depart! for ~~Cora~~ is not kind.

I saw a cloud of whitest hue;
Onward to the Moon it paſs'd!
Still brighter and more bright it grew
With floating colours not a few,
Till it reach'd the Moon at last.

MS. Sir John Murray

yon
~~Like the rays on the blue gushing stream~~
Oh snatched away in Beauty's bloom —
On thee shall preſs no ponderous tomb —
But on thy turf shall roses rear
    ir   *ves*
Their ~~tender~~ leaſ — the earliest of the year
And the wild cypreſs wave in gentle gloom.

2

  oft by
And yon blue-gushing ſtream
              lean her drooping head
Shall Sorrow ~~on the waters gaze~~
    deep
feed ~~her~~ thoughts   with many a dream
And ~~lost in deep remembrance dream~~
    & lingering
And ~~long shall~~ pause — and lightly tread —
     her footstep could
As if ~~her still fearful~~ to disturb the dead —

3 —

But
~~But thou for whom the loud lament~~
~~Was rais'd —~~ Oh ~~ever wept~~
         that tears are vain —
Away — we know ~~tis idle all~~ —
That death nor hears nor heeds distreſs —
Will this unteach us to complain
Or make one mourner weep the leſs —
  And
~~Even~~ thou who tell'st me to forget
Thy looks are wan — thine eyes are wet. —

MS. Ashley 5031, British Museum

Deep deep
A ~~deep deep~~ *wounds Adonis*
　A deeper Venus bears within her heart.
　See, his beloved Dogs are gathering round
　The Oread nymphs are weeping — Aphrodite
　~~*Loosening her hair is*~~
　　With hair unbound is *wandering thro the woods*
　　　　　　　　　　　　　　　　　　　　pierce
　　Wildered, ~~*ungirt*~~ *unsandalled* ~~*and*~~ *the thorns*
　　　　　hastening ~~*feet*~~
　　~~*Pierce*~~ *her,* ~~*coming*~~ *　　& drink her sacred blood*
　　　　　　　out
　　Bitterly screaming ~~*forth*~~ *she is driven on*
　　Thro the long vales; and her Afsyrian boy
　　Her love her husband calls — the purple blood
　　　　　　　　　　　　　　　　now
　　From her struck thigh stains her white navel ~~*snow*~~
　　Her bosom, and her neck before like snow

　~~*Alas*~~ *If*
　　　Alas for Cytherea — the loves mourn
　　　The lovely the beloved is gone — & now
　　　　Her
　　　~~*The*~~ *sacred beauty vanishes away.*
　　　For Venus whilst Adonis lived was fair
　　　Alas her lovelinefs is dead with him
　　　　oaks
　　　The ~~*moun*~~ *and mountains cry, ay ay Adonis!*
　　　　~~*rills their*~~ *their murmurs tears & groans*
　　　　　　　　　　　　　　　　　　　　　we
　　　The ~~*rivers*~~ *change　their* ~~*streams*~~ *to* ~~*tears*~~
　　　　springs
　　　　　their waters
　　　The springs ^　change ~~*their*~~ *to tears & weep*
　　　The flowers are withered up with grief

25

Ode to the Nightingale

My Heart aches and a drowsy numbness pains
My sense, as though of hemlock I had drunk,
Or emptied some dull opiate to the drains
One minute past and Lethe-wards had sunk:
'Tis not through envy of thy happy lot
But being too happy in thine happiness
That thou light-winged dryad of the trees
In some melodious plot
Of beechen green, and shadows numberless
Singest of summer in full-throated ease.

O for a draught of vintage that has been
Cooling an age in the deep-delved earth
Tasting of Flora, and the country green
Dance, and provencal song and sunburnt mirth
O for a Beaker full of the warm south,
Full of the true and blushful Hippocrene
With clustered bubbles winking at the brim
and purple-stained mouth
That I might drink and leave the world unseen
and with thee fade away into the forest dim

Fade far away dissolve and quite forget
What thou among the leaves hast never known
The weariness, the fever and the fret
Here, where men sit and hear each other groan
Where palsy shakes a few sad last grey hairs
Where youth grows pale and thin and dies

MS. Fitzwilliam Museum, Cambridge

26

Ode to the Nightingale

       drowsy
~~*My*~~ *Heart aches and a ~~painful~~ numbneſs ~~falls~~*
                              pains
My sense, as though of hemlock I had drunk
Or emptied some dull opiate to the drains
       past
One minute ~~hence~~ and Lethe-wards had sunk:
'Tis not through envy of thy happy lot,
But being too happy in thine happineſs,
That thou light-winged dryad of the trees
In some melodious plot
Of beechen green, and shadows numberleſs
Singest of summer in full-throated ease.
O for a draught of vintage that has been
         long
Cool~~ed~~ an age in the deep-delved earth
Tasting of Flora, and the country green
~~And~~ Dance, and provencal song and sunburnt mirth
O for a Beaker full of the warm South,
Full of the true and blushful Hippocrene
With cluster'd bubbles winking at the brim
And purple stained mouth,
That I might drink and leave the world unseen
And with thee fade away into the forest dim —
Fade far away, diſsolve and quite forget
What thou among the leaves hast never known
The wearineſs, the fever and the fret
Here, where Men sit and hear each other groan
Where palsy shakes a few sad last grey hairs
              spectre
Where youth grows pale and —thin ~~and old~~
                  and dies

Img)

If there were dreams to sell
 What wod you buy?
Some cost a kissing bell
Some a light sigh,
That shakes from Life's fresh crown
Only a rose leaf down.
 If there were dreams to sell,   Merry and sad to tell
  What would you buy?   and the crier rung the bell

A cottage lone & still
 With bowers nigh,
Shadowy, my woes to still
 Until I die,
Such pearl from life's fresh crown
 Fain would I shake me down
  If there were dreams to have at will
   This would I buy,   This would not please an ill
 But there were dreams to sell   best heal my
  Ill didst thou buy
 Life is a dream they tell,
  Waking, to die.
 Dreaming a dream to prize,
  Is wishing ghosts to rise —
 And if I had the spell   To raise call the ghosts a farewell,
  What ghost raised I?
 If there were ghosts to raise
  What shall I call,
 Out of hell's murky haze,
  Heaven's blue pall?
 Raise the loved longlost boy
  To lead me to his joy.
 There are no ghosts to raise   out of death lead no ways
  Vain is the call
 Know'st thou not ghosts to sue?
  No love thou hast
 Else lie as I will do   Thus are the ghosts to woo
   and breathe thy last   Thus are all dreams
 So out of life's fresh crown   made true
  Fall like a rose leaf down.   Ever to last

MS. 39674 f. 9b, British Museum

28

Song If there were dreams to sell
          What wd you buy?
      Some cost a passing bell
          Some a light sigh
      That shakes from life's fresh crown
          Only a roseleaf down.
              If there were dreams to sell   Merry and sad to tell
              What would you buy?   And the crier rung the bell

      A cottage lone & still
          With bowers nigh
      Shadowy, my woes to still
          Until I die
      Such pearl from life's fresh crown
          Fain would I shake me down
              ~~If there~~ Were dreams to have at will
                  This would I buy   This would ~~not please me~~ ill
                                      best heal my

      But there were dreams to sell
          Ill didst thou buy
      Life is a dream they tell:
          Waking, to die
      Dreaming a dream to prize
          Is wishing ghosts to rise —
      And if I had the spell,   ~~To raise call the ghosts up~~ well
          What ghost raised I?
                  ——

      If there were ghosts to raise
          What shall I call
      Out of hell's murky haze
              Heavens blue pall?

                  my
      Raise ~~the~~ loved longlost boy
          To lead me to his joy.
          There are no ghosts to raise
              Vain is the call   Out of death lead no ways
          Knowst thou not ghosts to sue?
              No love thou hast
          Else lie as I will do   Thus are the ghosts to woo
              And breathe thy last   Thus are all dreams
          So out of life's fresh crown   made true
              Fall like a rose leaf down.   Ever to last

29

Milton

Alcaics

—

O mighty-mouth'd inventor of harmonies,
~~Equal~~ to sing of Time or Eternity,
  O skill'd   God-gifted organ-voice of England,
      Milton, a name to resound for ages;
Whose Titan angels, Gabriel, Abdiel,
Stark'd from Jehovah's gorgeous armouries,
      Tower, as the deep-domed empyréan
        Rings to the roar of an angel onset—
Me rather all that bowery loneliness,
The brooks of Eden mazily murmuring,
      And bloom profuse & cedar arches
        Charm, as a wanderer out in ocean,
Where some refulgent sunset of India
~~Streams~~ o'er a rich ambrosial ocean isle,
  Streams   And crimson-hued the stately palmwoods
        Whisper in odorous heights of ~~Eden~~.
                              ever.

h:t is to be read as a dactyl, but as a trochee: its
long syllable; for the line is meant to be read
slowly.

2

Milton

—

Alcaics   .

—

O *mighty-mouth'd inventor of harmonies,*
  ~~Equal~~ *to sing of Time or Eternity,*
O *skill'd*
          God-gifted organ-voice of England,
              Milton, a name to resound for ages,
Whose Titan Angels, Gabriel, Abdiel,
     r'd
*Star*t *from Jehovah's gorgeous armouries,*
     Tower, as the deep-domed empyrëan
          Rings to the roar of an angel onset —
Me rather all that bowery loneliness,
Those brooks of Eden mazily murmuring,
     And bloom profuse & cedar arches
          Charm, as a wanderer out in ocean,
Where some refulgent sunset of India
          ~~*Dies*~~
~~*Streams*~~ *o'er a rich ambrosial ocean isle,*
     ~~*Dies*~~
(Streams /*And crimson-hued the stately palmwoods*
          Whisper in odorous heights of ~~*Eden.*~~
                    even.

*Not to be read as a dactyl, but as a trochee &
long syllable, for the line is meant to be read
slowly.*

31

MS. Add. 43486, British Museum

The priest,

~~How has~~, whose name she read when she would read

(feigned, false)   ~~therefore~~

Those ∧ letters ~~to me~~ I was forced to hear

Though I could read no word of, — he should cease

Writing, — nay, if he minded prayer of mine,

from   2   1

Cease ∧ so much even as pass down the street

Whereon our house looked, — in my ignorance

I was just thwarting Guido's true intent

Which was to bring about a wicked ~~know~~ change Of sport to earnest, tempt a thoughtless man

~~priest~~ ~~My friend should write~~ and pass the house, and more,

To write indeed,

Till both of us were taken in a ~~temp~~ crime.

He ought not to have wished me thus act lies,

folly,

Simulate ~~guilt~~, — but, wrong or right ~~of him~~, the wish,

apprehend its drift.

I failed to ~~take this the wish. Why then~~ How plain

It follows, — if I fell into such fault,

He also   the mark,

~~Why~~ may ~~not he~~ have over reached ~~himself~~

Made Mistaken, by perversity of brain,

sad strange

In the whole ∧ plot, ~~from first to last~~, this same intrigue

To make me and my friend unself ourselves,

Be other man and woman than we were!

Think it out, you who have the time! for me

I cannot ~~will~~ say less, (I will not say more;)   be

Leave it to God to cover and ~~forgive's~~ undo!

should

Only, my dulness ~~does~~ not prove ~~at all~~ too much,

other

That in a certain ~~single~~ point| — ~~wherein~~

me,

My husband blamed ∧ and you ~~who~~ blame

smiles and   was dull too, — oh   but

If I interpret ∧ shakes of head, | ~~aright, I did so very wrong~~, If I dared ∧ speak

Must I speak? I am blamed that I forwent

to

A way ~~had~~ make my husband's favour come.

That is true: I was firm, withstood, refused...

P.

not prove

wherein

MS. Ashley 2517, British Museum

We were black, we were black!
  We had no claim to love & bliſs
  What marvel, if each turned to lack?
~~So bliſs & love fill out to wrack~~
  They wrung my cold hands out of his —
They dragged him....why, I crawled to touch
  ~~The mark of his blood~~
~~His blood-mark~~ in the dust..not much
  His blood's mark
  Ye Pilgrim-souls,..though plain as this!

I am black, I am black —
  I wore a child
~~A child bearing~~ upon my breast..
An amulet that hung too slack
  And in my unrest could not rest —
    Thus we went moaning
And thus we moaned, we, child & mother,
One to another, one to another,
  Until all ended for the best,

For hark! I will tell you low.. low..
  I am black, you see, —
And the babe that lay on my bosom so,
  Was far too white..too white for me;
As white as the ladies who scorned to pray
Beside me at church but yesterday,
  Though my tears had washed a place for my knee

*[left margin, rotated:]* Wrong, followed by a deeper wrong! — / Grief seemed too good for such as I / So the white men brought the shame ere long / To stifle the sob in my throat thereby / They wᵈ not leave me for my dull / Wet eyes! — it was too merciful / To let me weep pure tears & die!

Love's
~~Beauty's~~ Compass (H. of L.)

Sometimes ~~thou~~ seemst not as thyself alone,
But as the meaning of all things that are;
A breathless wonder, shadowing forth afar
Some heavenly solstice hushed & halcyon;
Whose ~~un~~stirred lips are music's visible tone;
Whose eyes the ...... of the soul unbar,
Being .... furthest lives oracular; —
The ardent heart of all life's Sown & mown.

Even such Love is; and is not thy name Love?
Yea, by thy hand the Love-god lends apart
All gathering clouds of Nights ambiguous art;
Flings them far down, & sets thine eyes above;
And simply, as some gage of flower or glove,
Stakes with a smile the world against thy heart.

MS. Add. 34813.3, British Museum

Sleeping at last, the trouble & tumult over,
Sleeping at last, the struggle & horror past,
Cold & white out of sight of friend & of lover
Sleeping at last.
No more a tired heart downcast or overcast,
No more pangs that wring or shifting fears that hover,
Sleeping at last in a dreamless sleep locked fast.
Fast asleep. Singing birds in their leafy cover
Cannot wake her; nor shake her the gusty blast.
Under the purple thyme & the purple clover
Sleeping at last.

MS. Add. 34813, British Museum

Love's ~~Secret~~
~~Beauty's~~ Compaſs (H. of L.)

  thou   thyself
Sometimes ~~you~~ seemst not as ~~yourself~~ alone,
 But as the meaning of all things that are;
 A breathleſs wonder, shadowing forth afar
Some heavenly solstice hushed & halcyon;
Whose ~~still~~ unstirred lips are music's visible tone;
   ~~dawn gate~~ sun-gate
 Whose eyes the ~~silence~~ of the soul unbar,
   ~~with~~ of ~~the~~ its
 Being ~~made of~~ ∧ furthest fires oracular; —
    life
The evident heart of all ~~things~~ sown & mown.

Even such Love is;
~~Is Love not there~~; and is not thy name Love?
 Yea, by thy hand the Love-god rends apart
 All gathering clouds of Night's ambiguous art;
Flings them far down, & sets thine eyes above;
And simply, as some gage of flower or glove,
 Stakes with a smile the world against thy heart.

Sleeping at last, the trouble & tumult over,
Sleeping at last, the struggle & horror past,
Cold & white out of sight of friend & of lover
Sleeping at last.
   a
No more a tired heart downcast or overcast,
No more pangs that wring or shifting fears that hover,
Sleeping at last in a dreamleſs sleep locked fast.
Fast asleep. Singing birds in their leafy cover
Cannot wake her, nor shake her the gusty blast.
Under the purple thyme & the purple clover
Sleeping at last.

over

37

MS. Ashley A 1851, British Museum

Three days' love between us,
And then a three nights' dream
Take hands & part with laughter,
Touch lips & part with tears;
We shall not
Once more & no more after,
For all the mournful
YW Whatever comes with years
We twain shall not remeasure
                    left
The ways that ~~made~~ us twain;
once more
~~Take hands~~ with pleasure
Nor crush the wine of
              From sanguine grapes of
Touch lips once more with pain
Remembrance may recover
And time bring back to time
The name of your first lover,
The ring of my first rhyme;
And June may kiss December
~~And~~ roses of November
                    shall
But the frost of ~~May~~ June ~~may~~ fret;
The day that you
But what can love remember ?
The day that I
And what can time forget?
Time found our tired
Our three days love ~~lies bleeding~~ sleeping
        kiss fierce   kissed & away,
                        kissed such
        Time   draws his breath;
        sucks kiss had choked
        And *touched & quenched*
Ev But what shd we do weeping
Tho' light love sleep to death?
We have drained his lips at leisure,
Till there's not left to drain
        sob of
A single ~~tear~~ for pleasure
        for
        shiver &
A single ~~smile for~~ pain.
        pulse for

If you
The parting laugh
Lips &
(Question)
Not Her absence of flesh but the pretence of spirit is admirable or adorable

We have seen
The laughter of We have such the veiled fair faces
And That love turns doubtful in
We have seen face's heart
Talk
looks
trod the dusty strange places
waste
seen
That know what
That time

Rococo

39

The Starlight Night — Sonnet

Look at the stars! look, look up at the skies!
O look at all the fire-folk sitting in the air!
The bright boroughs, the quivering citadels there!
Look, the elf-rings; look at the out round earger eyes
The grey lawns cold where quaking gold-dew lies!
Wind-beat whitebeam, airy abeles all on flare!
Flake-doves sent floating out at a farmyard scare! —
Ah well! It is a purchase and a prize.

Buy then! Bid then! — What? — Prayer, patience, alms, vows. *Rall.*

Look, look — a May-mess, like on orchard boughs!
Look — March-bloom, like on mealed-with-yellow sallows!
These are the barn, indeed: within doors house
The shocks. This pale and parclose hides the spouse
Christ and the mother of Christ and all His Hallows.

Feb. 24

---

*The dim woods quick with diamond wells, the elf-eyes!
The diamond wells through dim woods quick, the elf-eyes!

† The shocks. This day-shot paling hides the spouse.
The shocks. This pierced-well paling hides the spouse
The shocks. This piece-bright

The bright boroughs, the silver citadels there;
The diamond wells quick in dim woods, the elf-eyes;
dim woods
through dim woods the elf-eyes;
The grey lawns cold where jaunting gold-dew lies
The grey lawns cold jaunting there gold-dew lies;
The grey lawns cold, jaunting where gold-dew lies;

MS. The Bodleian Library, Oxford

The Starlight Night — Sonnet

Look at the stars! look, look up at the skies!
   O
  ~~Lo~~ look at all the fire-folk sitting in the air!
  The bright boroughs, the quivering citadels there!
*~~Look, the elf-rings; look at the out-round eager eyes!~~
          where
The grey lawns cold ~~qua~~ quaking gold-dew lies!

  Wind-beat whitebeam, airy abeles all on flare!
  Flake-doves sent floating out at a farmyard
         scare! —
Ah well! It is a purchase and a prize.
               Rall.
Buy then! Bid then! — what? — Prayer, patience,
      alms, vows. —
  Look, look — a May-mess, like on orchard boughs!
  Look — March-bloom, like on mealed-with-yel-
      low sallows!
These are the barn, indeed: within doors house
†The shocks. This pale and parclose hides the
         spouse
  Christ and the Mother of Christ and all His
      Hallows.
           Feb, 24

* { The dim woods quick with diamond wells; the elf-eyes!
  { The diamond wells through dim woods quick, the elf-eyes!

† The shocks. This day-shot paling hides the Spouse
   The shocks. This pierced — well paling hides the spouse
   The shocks. This piece-bright —   —   —   —

The bright boroughs, the silver citadels there;
           in
The diamond wells quick ~~in~~ dim woods; the elf eyes;
      ~~down dim woods~~
          through dim woods; the elf eyes;
The grey lawns cold where jaunting gold ~~dew~~ dew lies
          there
{ The grey lawns cold jaunting, ~~for~~ gold dew lies;

{ The grey lawns cold, jaunting where gold dew lies;

41

MS. 44990. 641f, British Museum

Adlestrop

Yes, I remember Adlestrop —
At least the name. One afternoon
    the express train
Of heat ~~the train slowed down~~ drew up there
  Against its custom It'|was June.
~~There unexpectedly.~~

Yes, I remember Adlestrop —
  The name, because
~~At least the name.~~ One afternoon
Of heat, the express train drew up there
~~Against its custom~~
Unwontedly. It was late June.

The steam hissed. Someone cleared his throat.
No one left & no one came
On the bare platform. What I saw
Was Adlestrop, only the name,

And, willows, willow herb & grass,
And meadowsweet. The haycocks dry
Were not less still & lonely fair
Than the high cloudlets ~~tiers~~ in the sky

And all that minute a blackbird sang
Close by, and round him, mistier,
Farther & farther, all the birds
Of Oxfordshire & Gloucestershire.

43

MS. King's College, Cambridge

once   *love*
Gave, of her flowers to pick, her ways to roam

(& fed by her & shaped)
     an English   HOOD BATTALION,
Who breathed her air   *streams*   2nd NAVAL BRIGADE,
    washed by the waves of home   BLANDFORD,
    rivers   DORSET.
washed by the rivers

   If I should die think/of me/only this
       there's
     That ~~in~~ some corner of a foreign field
   ~~*Something of England lies*~~   *(is)*
   That is for ever England   *There shall be*
   In that rich earth a richer dust ~~ten~~ concealed
   A dust whom England bore, shaped, made aware,
   Gav
   Who ate her food, who breathed an English air

    And think
   ~~*Think too, this heart, all evil shed away,*~~
   Think, too, this heart, all evil shed away,
   An 'obscure pulse in the Eternal mind,
   Gives some where back the thoughts (that England gave.)
   Thoughts   *dreams happy as her day*
       thought,
Content

Anthem for Dead Youth.

What passing-bells for these who die so fast?
— Only the monstrous anger of our guns
Let the majestic insults of their mouths
Be as the priest-words of their burials.
Of choristers and holy music, none;
Nor any voice of mourning save the wail
The long drawn wail of high far sailing shells.

What candles may we hold for these lost souls?
— Not in the hands of boys, but in their eyes
Shall many flames
And women's wide-spreaded arms shall be their wreaths,
And pallor of girls cheeks shall be their palls.
Their flowers, the tenderness of minds,
And Dusk, a drawing-down of blinds.

First Draft
(With Sassoon's amendments.)

MS. Add. 43721, British Museum

Anthem for Dead Youth

     passing
What ~~minute~~ bells for these who die so fast?
      (~~solemn~~   the
— Only the { monstrous anger of ~~our~~ guns.
   blind insolence   *iron*
Let the ~~majestic insults~~ of ~~their iron~~ mouths
      requiem .
  Be as the ~~priest-words~~ of their ~~burials~~ —
  Learn   organs for the old   *requiem*
~~Of~~ choristers and holy music, *none;*
  Nor any voice of mourning, save the wail
And the   *hiss.* *lonely*
~~The~~ long- ~~drawn wail~~ of ~~high far~~ -sailing shells.
             to light
  What candles may we hold ~~for~~ these lost? ~~souls?~~
—Not in the hands of boys, but in their eyes
    shine the ~~tapers~~   *the holy* ~~tapers~~.. *candles*
Shall ʌ many ~~candles; shine; and Love will light them~~.
     ~~holy~~ *flames: to*
And Women's wide-spread~~ed~~ arms shall be their wreaths,
  And pallor of girls' cheeks shall be their palls.

            ~~mortal~~
  Their flowers, the tenderness of ~~all men's~~ minds
           ~~comrades'~~
          rough mens

   each slow
And ~~every~~ Dusk, a drawing-down of blinds.

         First ~~Draught~~ Draft
       (*With Sassoon's amendments.*)

He is ~~beautiful~~
His
Moses is ~~inexperienced~~
His ~~love~~ of pleasure his pleasure in
~~Ferocious~~ in the earnestness mastery
~~Ambition~~ bring himself & us to ruin
We will suffer more
— They suspect him already

Old Hebrew to himself.   His youth is flattered at
                                        Moses kind speech to him
~~His~~

To the young Hel.   I am broken &   have
                              ~~I have grown~~ grey,   & seen much
                                                              in my time
                      And all this gay grotesque of
                      glory   childish ~~pain~~
                      ~~his~~ past itself   ~~&~~ I grumble that
                                   I half blind half deaf   I only
                      I am not blind or deaf   grumble
                      I have seen splendid fools   experience
                      Into a prophets ~~throne~~   I heard themselves
                      So many crazed shadows puffed away.
                      And conscious cheats with such an
        Mouthed in the eyes   They ed make a bonfire of themselves for fame
        & read in the   in the public
        Public eye   Mouthed the ~~prices~~   in the public ~~that~~
                                        Moses loves pleasure,   his pleasure in
                                 This prince
His wild flesh is his ~~sin~~   Ferocious & this will mastery
                          To ~~...~~   unsafe & ~~...~~
        Egyptian ~~...~~ trust in   Egypt suspect Short of terror
                   ~~Moses abroad~~   follow him ~~...~~

MS. 48210, British Museum

He is ~~lustful~~
~~His f~~
Moses is ~~inexperienced~~
His love of pleasure his pleasure in
                              mastery
        Ferocious in the earnestness of self
~~Abnegation~~ bring himself & us to ruin
              ~~Will~~
        only
        We will suffer more
        ~~They suspect him already~~
Old Hebrew to himself. His youth is flattered at
        His   Moses kind speech to him
                      am broken &   have
      To the young Heb   I ~~have grown~~ grey & seen much
                                    in my time
                    And all this gay grotesque of
                    Long   childish man
                    ~~Ive past, it all & all I grumbled at~~
                        half blind half deaf I only
                                        grumble
                                            now
                    I am not blind or deaf enough for peace
                                    young
                    I have seen splendid fools
                                        cheat themselves
                    Into a prophets frenzy, I have seen
                    So many crazed shadows puffed away
                    And concious cheats with such an
                                        ich for fame
Mouthed in the squares   Theyed make a bonfire of themselves
broad in the   ~~in the public eye~~
public eye   Mouthed the squares   ~~rather~~
                                        to be
                              in the public eye,
                    ~~Moses~~ loves pleasure, his pleasure in
              This prince   mastery
                              & ~~his will~~
                    Ferocious & ~~tenacious~~
His wild flesh is his ruin   unsafe & ~~full~~
                                        of
            ~~To those~~ at play   shot with terror
                    Trust in   Eypt suspects him now
          ~~Egyptian~~ woman
                    Heres Abinoah follows him about

4   49   SPC

II

THE POET'S
PRINTED REVISIONS

1

Bid me but live, and I will live
    Thy Votary to be:
Or bid me love, and I will give
    A loving heart to thee.

A heart as soft, a heart as kind,
    A heart as soundly free,
As in the world thou canst not find,
    That heart Ile give to thee.

Bid that heart stay, and it shall stay,
    And honour thy Decree:
Or bid it languish quite away,
    And it shall do't so for thee.

Bid me to weep, and I will weep,
    While I have eyes to see:
Or having none, yet I will keep
    A heart to weep for thee.

Thou art my life, my love, my heart,
    The very eye of me:
And hast command of every part,
    To live and die for thee.

This song by Robert Herrick was set to music by Henry Lawes, and appeared in a music-book *Select Musicall Ayres and Dialogues*, published by John Playford in 1652.

It also appears in the *Hesperides*, published in 1648, under the title *TO ANTHEA, who may command him any thing*. We know that many of Herrick's songs in Playford's music-books were based upon manuscript versions which are really early drafts of the poems. So we may be fairly certain that the Hesperides version is the correct and final text, and the one given above a reprint of one of these earlier drafts.

Here is the *Hesperides* text of this well-known poem for purpose of comparison. One must remark on the more arresting opening the reader may consider the variant readings himself, and decid upon the fifth stanza, which does not appear in the song-book.

TO ANTHEA, who may command him any thing

1 Bid me to live, and I will live
  Thy Protestant to be:
 Or bid me love, and I will give
  A loving heart to thee.

2 A heart as soft, a heart as kind,
  A heart as sound and free,
 As in the whole world thou canst find,
  That heart Ile give to thee.

3 Bid that heart stay, and it will stay,
  To honour thy Decree:
 Or bid it languish quite away,
  And't shall doe so for thee.

4 Bid me to weep, and I will weep,
  While I have eyes to see:
 And having none, yet I will keep
  A heart to weep for thee.

5 Bid me despaire, and Ile despaire,
  Under that *Cypresse* tree:
 Or bid me die, and I will dare
  E'en Death, to die for thee.

6 Thou art my life, my love, my heart,
  The very eyes of me:
 And hast command of every part,
  To live and die for thee.

2

Goldsmith's most famous poem, *The Deserted Village*, was en-
thusiastically received when it first appeared in May, 1770. The
pictures in which it excels are the result of the poet's accurate
observation. He was storing his mind with descriptions many years
before the poem was written. Occasionally, he expressed himself in
a rough draft, or in a letter, and made use of the passage in a modi-
fied form in his greater work. Here is his description of an Author's
Bedchamber. It comes from a letter written to his brother, the
Rev. Henry Goldsmith, in 1759, which Goldsmith begins:

Your last letter, I repeat it, was too short: you should have given
me your opinion of the design of the heroicomical poem which I sent
you: you remember I intended to introduce the hero of the poem,
as lying in a paltry alehouse. You may take the following specimen
of the manner, which I flatter myself is quite original. The room in
which he lies, may be described somewhat in this way:

> The window, patch'd with paper, lent a ray,
> That feebly shew'd the state in which he lay.
> The sanded floor, that grits beneath the tread:
> The humid wall with paltry pictures spread;
> The game of goose was there expos'd to view
> And the twelve rules the royal martyr drew:
> The seasons, fram'd with listing, found a place,
> And Prussia's monarch shew'd his lamp-black face.
> The morn was cold; he views with keen desire,
> A rusty grate unconscious of a fire.
> An unpaid reck'ning on the frieze was scor'd,
> And five crack'd tea-cups dress'd the chimney board.

These lines appear, with a few alterations, in Letter XXX of *The
Citizen of the World*, published in 1762. They are read aloud at a
club of authors by a poet in 'shabby finery', who asserts that he had
composed them the day before, and explains his design in these
words: 'The poem begins with the description of an author's bed-

chamber: the picture was sketched in my own apartment; for you must know, gentlemen, that I am myself the hero.' Then putting himself into the attitude of an orator, with all the emphasis of voice and action, he proceeds:

'Where the Red Lion flaring o'er the way,
 Invites each passing stranger that can pay;
 Where Calvert's butt, and Parson's black champagne,
 Regale the drabs and bloods of Drury-Lane;
 There in a lonely room, from bailiffs snug,
 The Muse found Scroggen stretch'd beneath a rug;
 A window patch'd with paper lent a ray,
 That dimly show'd the state in which he lay;
 The sanded floor that grits beneath the tread;
 The humid wall with paltry pictures spread:
 The royal game of goose was there in view,
 And the twelve rules the royal martyr drew;
 The seasons, fram'd with listing, found a place,
 And brave prince William show'd his lamp-black face:
 The morn was cold, he views with keen desire
 The rusty grate unconscious of a fire;
 With beer and milk arrears the frieze was scor'd,
 And five crack'd teacups dress'd the chimney board;
 A nightcap deck'd his brows instead of bay,
 A cap by night—a stocking all the day!'

From this second version Goldsmith adapted his description of the inn parlour in *The Deserted Village*:

Low lies that house where nut-brown draughts inspir'd,
Where grey-beard mirth and smiling toil retir'd,
Where village statesmen talk'd with looks profound,
And news much older than their ale went round.
Imagination fondly stoops to trace
The parlour splendours of that festive place;
The white-wash'd wall, the nicely-sanded floor,
The varnish'd clock that click'd behind the door;
The chest contriv'd a double debt to pay,
A bed by night, a chest of drawers by day;

> The pictures plac'd for ornament and use,
> The twelve good rules, the royal game of goose;
> The hearth, except when winter chill'd the day,
> With aspen boughs, and flowers, and fennel, gay;
> While broken tea-cups, wisely kept for show,
> Rang'd o'er the chimney, glisten'd in a row.

One may almost trace the changes in Goldsmith's fortunes by comparing these three versions. When he submitted to his brother Henry a sample of a heroi-comic poem describing a Grub Street writer lying in a 'paltry alehouse', he was himself living miserably in the squalor of Green Arbour Court, Old Bailey. Soon, however, his fortunes began to mend. He published his periodical *The Bee*, contributed to various magazines, and was employed by John Newbery, the publisher. He made the acquaintance of Garrick and Johnson, and was one of the original members of 'The Club'.

The second version of the poem first appeared in Newbery's *Public Ledger* in one of the series of 'Chinese Letters', subsequently published as *The Citizen of the World*. The scene has now become the Red Lion in Drury Lane. The poem is changed slightly to suit the occasion—the description of the proceedings of the club of authors, most of whom do not wish to hear the first book of an heroic poem read by one of their number. In spite of this the poet holds forth, and when he reaches the last line he cries, 'there is a description for you; Rabelais's bedchamber is but a fool to it.

> A cap by night—a stocking all the day!

There is sound, and sense, and truth, and nature in the trifling compass of ten little syllables.'

This line has its parallel in the adapted version in *The Deserted Village*, where a piece of furniture pays a double debt—

> A bed by night, a chest of drawers by day.

Once again Goldsmith's circumstances have changed, and produced their changes in the poem. He is no longer a Grub Street writer. Unharassed by poverty, he casts his mind back to Sweet Auburn. Distance adds its own charm to the scene. The village inn has no windows 'patch'd with paper', or 'humid walls', or empty grate. Instead we have

> The parlour splendours of that festive place,

shown further in 'the white-wash'd wall' and 'the varnish'd clock'. But certain accessories are retained: 'the sanded floor', the 'twelve good rules', the pictures, no longer paltry, but 'plac'd for ornament and use', the tea-cups, now broken, are 'wisely kept for show'. The hearth is filled with 'aspen boughs and flowers, and fennel gay'. This inn parlour is a pleasant place; but it derives from the description of a 'paltry ale-house' written twelve years before.

3

The poplars are fell'd and adieu to the shade
And the whispering sound of the cool colonnade,
Their winds play no longer and sing in the leaves,
Nor Ouse in its bosom their image receives.

Twelve years had elaps'd since I last took a view
Of my favourite field and the bank where they grew,
When behold on their sides in the grass they were laid,
And I sat on the trees under which I had stray'd.

The blackbird has sought out another retreat
Where the hazels afford him a screen from the heat,
And the scene where his notes have oft charm'd me before,
Shall resound with his sweet-flowing ditty no more.

My fugitive years are all hast'ning away,
And I must alas! lie as lowly as they,
With a turf on my breast, and a stone at my head,
Ere another such grove rises up in its stead.

The change both my heart and my fancy employs,
I reflect on the frailty of man, and his joys;
Short-lived as we are, yet our pleasures, we see,
Have a still shorter date, and die sooner than we.

William Cowper wrote *The Poplar-Field* in 1784, and it was published, as above, in *The Gentleman's Magazine* in January of the following year. As a result of some friendly criticism, the poem was considerably altered, and was afterwards published in 1800 in this revised version:

> The poplars are fell'd farewell to the shade
> And the whispering sound of the cool colonnade,
> The winds play no longer, and sing in the leaves,
> Nor Ouse on his bosom their image receives.
>
> Twelve years have elaps'd since I first took a view
> Of my favourite field and the bank where they grew,
> And now in the grass behold they are laid,
> And the tree is my seat that once lent me a shade.
>
> The blackbird has fled to another retreat
> Where the hazels afford him a screen from the heat,
> And the scene where his melody charm'd me before,
> Resounds with his sweet-flowing ditty no more.
>
> My fugitive years are all hasting away,
> And I must ere long lie as lowly as they,
> With a turf on my breast, and a stone at my head,
> Ere another such grove shall arise in its stead.
>
> 'Tis a sight to engage me, if any thing can,
> To muse on the perishing pleasures of man;
> Though his life be a dream, his enjoyments, I see,
> Have a being less durable even than he.

The reader may consider why the changes were made, and whether the poem in its revised form is an improvement or not.

4

We all know Wordsworth's poem *The Daffodils*, which makes the sparkling scene live for us again. Anyone would imagine it to be the spontaneous description of a memorable occasion. But the immediate account of that April scene was written in Dorothy Wordsworth's *Journal*, in unstudied prose, which you may consider to be as lovely as her brother's lyric. They were returning together from Eusemere to Dove Cottage.

When we were in the woods beyond Gowbarrow Park we saw a few daffodils close to the water-side. We fancied that the lake had floated the seeds ashore, and that the little colony had so sprung up. But as we went along there were more and yet more; and at last, under the boughs of the trees, we saw that there was a long belt of them along the shore, about the breadth of a country turnpike road. I never saw daffodils so beautiful. They grew among the mossy stones about and about them; some rested their heads upon these stones as on a pillow for weariness; and the rest tossed and reeled and danced, and seemed as if they verily laughed with the wind, that blew upon them over the lake: they looked so gay, ever glancing, ever changing. This wind blew directly over the lake to them. There was here and there a little knot, and a few stragglers a few yards higher up, but they were so few as not to disturb the simplicity, unity and life of that one busy highway.

This was written on 15 April 1802. It was two years later that Wordsworth recorded the incident in verse. He may have 'recollected the scene in tranquillity', or he may have read the description in his sister's *Journal* and thus recalled the walk back to Grasmere, and 'the long belt' of daffodils, by the water-side. The poem was not published till 1807, and then not as we know it today. It had three verses.

> I wandered lonely as a cloud
> That floats on high o'er vales and hills,
> When all at once I saw a crowd,
> A host, of dancing daffodils;

Beside the lake, beneath the trees,
Fluttering and dancing in the breeze.

The waves beside them danced; but they
Out-did the sparkling waves in glee:
A poet could not but be gay,
In such a laughing company:
I gazed—and gazed—but little thought
What wealth the show to me had brought:

For oft when on my couch I lie
In vacant or in pensive mood,
They flash upon that inward eye
Which is the bliss of solitude;
And then my heart with pleasure fills,
And dances with the daffodils.

The two lines:

They flash upon that inward eye
Which is the bliss of solitude;

were by Mrs Wordsworth. They were said by Wordsworth to be
the two best lines in the poem'.

He revised the poem, making two alterations; the word 'golden'
was substituted for 'dancing' in line 4, and 'jocund' for 'laughing'
in line 10. He wrote another stanza, which was placed second in the
version published in 1815, the version which was to become so
universally known.

I wandered lonely as a cloud
That floats on high o'er vales and hills,
When all at once I saw a crowd,
A host, of golden daffodils;
Beside the lake, beneath the trees
Fluttering and dancing in the breeze.

Continuous as the stars that shine
And twinkle on the milky way,
They stretched in never-ending line
Along the margin of a bay:
Ten thousand saw I at a glance,
Tossing their heads in sprightly dance.

The waves beside them danced; but they
Out-did the sparkling waves in glee:
A poet could not but be gay,
In such a jocund company:
I gazed—and gazed—but little thought
What wealth the show to me had brought:

For oft, when on my couch I lie
In vacant or in pensive mood,
They flash upon that inward eye
Which is the bliss of solitude;
And then my heart with pleasure fills,
And dances with the daffodils.

This, I think we shall agree, is an improvement. Wordsworth ha
suggested the landscape, bare and austere, by comparing his ow
loneliness with that of a cloud floating over vales and hills. We ar
merely told of the lake and trees. The daffodils provide the ga
company amid this winter scene. They are the heralds, telling o
the invasion of Spring, bursting upon the poet like an army. Th
very economy of epithets makes the word 'golden' enhance th
pictorial effect still more, giving that warmth of colour which make
the scene leap to the eye. 'Dancing daffodils' as the original versio
had it, though pleasant in sound, would weaken the last line—

Fluttering and dancing in the breeze.

The second stanza adds much to the poem. We can already se
the daffodils as a host, by the water-side, underneath the trees. Thi
presents that unforgettable picture of the 'long belt of them alon
the shore, about the breadth of a country turnpike road'. Th
comparison with the stars on the milky way is happy and appropriate
it enlarges the imagination, giving radiance as well as number. I
connects the great sweep of the stars with the arresting line o
flowers, and combines the crystal freshness with twinkling move
ment. The eye follows the 'tossing heads' along that far margin
If the poem were without this stanza we should lose the spaciousnes
of the scene, the completeness of the picture.

The word 'laughing' in line 10 of the first version reminds us of Dorothy's description; the change to 'jocund' suggests that the flowers expressed their joy completely in the sparkling movement of the dance. Sound, even of laughter, does not intrude upon the scene. The final effect of the poem is one of joyful motion, which can fill the heart with pleasure.

When we consider how the poem was composed, we can say that three people had a hand in it. And even this delightful lyric, spontaneous as it may appear, was not written with that immediacy which one so often associates with poetic creation.

5

The Ancient Mariner, Coleridge's finest poem, was first planned, and in part composed, during a memorable walk begun on the afternoon of 13 November 1797. Dorothy Wordsworth gave him continual encouragement during the early months of 1798; and on 23 March he brought the poem to her at last completed.

It was published in the volume of *Lyrical Ballads* in the following September by Joseph Cottle at Bristol. It is entitled *The Rime of the Ancyent Marinere, in Seven Parts*, and is the first poem in the original octavo edition.

Here is a literal reprint of Part III from the first edition:

III

I saw a something in the Sky
  No bigger than my fist;
At first it seem'd a little speck
  And then it seem'd a mist:
It mov'd and mov'd, and took at last
  A certain shape, I wist.

A speck, a mist, a shape, I wist!
  And still it ner'd and ner'd;
And, an it dodg'd a water-sprite,
  It plung'd and tack'd and veer'd.

63

With throat unslack'd, with black lips bak'd
    Ne could we laugh, ne wail:
Then while thro' drouth all dumb they stood
I bit my arm and suck'd the blood
    And cry'd, A sail! a sail!

With throat unslack'd, with black lips bak'd
    Agape they hear'd me call:
Gramercy! they for joy did grin
And all at once their breath drew in
    As they were drinking all.

She doth not tack from side to side—
    Hither to work us weal
Withouten wind, withouten tide
    She steddies with upright keel.

The western wave was all a flame,
    The day was well nigh done!
Almost upon the western wave
    Rested the broad bright Sun;
When that strange shape drove suddenly
    Betwixt us and the Sun.

And strait the Sun was fleck'd with bars
    (Heaven's mother send us grace)
As if thro' a dungeon grate he peer'd
    With broad and burning face.

Alas! (thought I, and my heart beat loud)
    How fast she neres and neres!
Are those *her* Sails that glance in the Sun
    Like restless gossameres?

Are these *her* naked ribs, which fleck'd
    The sun that did behind them peer?
And are these two all, all the crew,
    That woman and her fleshless Pheere?

His bones were black with many a crack,
    All black and bare, I ween;

Jet-black and bare, save where with rust
Of mouldy damps and charnel crust
   They're patch'd with purple and green.

Her lips are red, *her* looks are free,
   Her locks are yellow as gold:
Her skin is as white as leprosy,
And she is far liker Death than he;
   Her flesh makes the still air cold.

The naked Hulk alongside came
   And the Twain were playing dice;
'The Game is done! I've won, I've won!'
   Quoth she, and whistled thrice.

A gust of wind sterte up behind
   And whistled thro' his bones;
Thro' the holes of his eyes and the hole of his mouth
   Half-whistles and half-groans.

With never a whisper in the Sea
   Off darts the Spectre-ship;
While clombe above the Eastern bar
The horned Moon, with one bright Star
   Almost atween the tips.

One after one by the horned Moon
   (Listen, O Stranger! to me)
Each turn'd his face with a ghastly pang
   And curs'd me with his ee.

Four times fifty living men,
   With never a sigh or groan,
With heavy thump, a lifeless lump
   They dropp'd down one by one.

Their souls did from their bodies fly,—
   They fled to bliss or woe;
And every soul it pass'd me by,
   Like the whiz of my Cross-bow.

The text was revised in 1800, 1802, 1805, and 1817. Here is the same passage in the final version, as given in 1817 in *Sibylline Leaves*:

III

There passed a weary time. Each throat
Was parched, and glazed each eye.
A weary time! a weary time!
How glazed each weary eye,
When looking westward, I beheld
A something in the sky.

At first it seemed a little speck,
And then it seemed a mist;
It moved and moved, and took at last
A certain shape, I wist.

A speck, a mist, a shape, I wist!
And still it neared and neared:
As if it dodged a water-sprite,
It plunged and tacked and veered.

With throats unslaked, with black lips baked,
We could nor laugh nor wail;
Through utter drought all dumb we stood!
I bit my arm, I sucked the blood,
And cried, A sail! a sail!

With throats unslaked, with black lips baked,
Agape they heard me call:
Gramercy! they for joy did grin,
And all at once their breath drew in,
As they were drinking all.

See! see! (I cried) she tacks no more!
Hither to work us weal;
Without a breeze, without a tide,
She steadies with upright keel!

The western wave was all a-flame.
The day was well nigh done!
Almost upon the western wave
Rested the broad bright Sun;

When that strange shape drove suddenly
Betwixt us and the Sun.

And straight the Sun was flecked with bars,
(Heaven's Mother send us grace!)
As if through a dungeon-grate he peered
With broad and burning face.

Alas! (thought I, and my heart beat loud)
How fast she nears and nears!
Are those *her* sails that glance in the Sun,
Like restless gossameres?

Are those *her* ribs through which the Sun
Did peer, as through a grate?
And is that Woman all her crew?
Is that a DEATH? and are there two?
Is DEATH that woman's mate?

Her lips were red, *her* looks were free,
Her locks were as yellow as gold:
Her skin was as white as leprosy,
The Night-mare LIFE-IN-DEATH was she,
Who thicks man's blood with cold.

The naked hulk alongside came,
And the twain were casting dice;
'The game is done! I've won! I've won!'
Quoth she, and whistles thrice.

The Sun's rim dips; the stars rush out:
At one stride comes the dark;
With far-heard whisper, o'er the sea,
Off shot the spectre-bark.

We listened and looked sideways up!
Fear at my heart, as at a cup,
My life-blood seemed to sip!
The stars were dim, and thick the night,
The steersman's face by his lamp gleamed white;
From the sails the dew did drip—
Till clomb above the eastern bar
The horned Moon, with one bright star
Within the nether tip.

5-2

One after one, by the star-dogged Moon,
Too quick for groan or sigh,
Each turned his face with a ghastly pang
And cursed me with his eye.

Four times fifty living men,
(And I heard nor sigh nor groan)
With heavy thump, a lifeless lump,
They dropped down one by one.

The souls did from their bodies fly,—
They fled to bliss or woe!
And every soul, it passed me by,
Like the whizz of my cross-bow!

Why did Coleridge make so many corrections in the subsequent editions of *The Ancient Mariner*? It is worth our consideration, in regard to craftsmanship, because every correction, and omission, improved the poem. Had he been quite satisfied that the poem which he brought to Dorothy Wordsworth was the final form which his inspiration could take, we should have a much less perfect poem than we have today. Some of the finest lines have been built up from unimpressive lines in the 1798 version. It has been said that the Romantic poets were not sound critics of their own work. This is not true of Coleridge in respect of *The Ancient Mariner*. When the poem was adversely received, he scrupulously revised it, and the results of that revision can be judged by comparing the two versions of Section III given above.

The severe handling which the poem received was due very largely to Southey. No doubt the quarrel over pantisocracy still rankled, and Southey took the opportunity to show his feelings when the *Lyrical Ballads* appeared. A few days after their publication, he wrote to William Taylor of Norwich:

Have you seen a volume of *Lyrical Ballads*? They are by Coleridge and Wordsworth, but their names are not affixed. Coleridge's *Ballad of the Ancyent Marinere* is, I think, the clumsiest attempt at German sublimity I ever saw. Many of the others are very fine;

and some I shall re-read upon the same principle that led me through Trissino, whenever I am afraid of writing like a child or an old woman.

About the same time as this letter, his review of the *Lyrical Ballads* was published in the *Critical Review* of October 1798. In this he says:

In a very different style of poetry is the *Rime of the Ancient Mariner*; a ballad (says the advertisement) 'professedly written in imitation of the *style*, as well as the spirit of the elder poets'. We are tolerably conversant with the early English poets; and can discover no resemblance whatever, except in antiquated spelling and a few obsolete words. This piece appears to us perfectly original in style as well as in story. Many of the stanzas are laboriously beautiful; but in connection they are absurd or unintelligible....We do not sufficiently understand the story to analyse it. It is a Dutch attempt at German sublimity. Genius has here been employed in producing a poem of little merit.

It is obvious that the reviewers of the first edition of the *Lyrical Ballads* took their line of attack from Southey's article, especially in regard to Coleridge's poem. One critic says, of the *Ancient Mariner*, 'We are not pleased with it; in our opinion it has more of the extravagance of a mad German poet, than of the simplicity of our ancient ballad writers....'

We find even Wordsworth writing to Cottle in 1799:

From what I can gather it seems that the *Ancient Mariner* has, on the whole, been an injury to the volume. I mean that the old words and the strangeness of it have deterred readers from going on. If the volume should come to a second edition, I would put in its place some little things which would be more likely to suit the common taste.

It is not surprising that Coleridge set about revising the poem. The tone of the reviewers underwent a gradual change; though critics still persisted in fault finding, they remarked on the beauties of the poem also. The *British Critic*, in October 1799, remarks that the beginning and the end 'are striking and well-conducted', but the middle part is 'confused' and 'not quite intelligible'. The language is criticized as incorrect, and in places 'nonsensical'; 'but the ancient style is well imitated, while the antiquated words are so very few, that the latter might with advantage be entirely removed without detriment to the effect of the Poem.'

Coleridge profited from all these comments, for the final version of the poem is free from many of the original archaisms; he also diminished much of the grotesqueness, the realism, and horror, and reduced some of the iteration of the 1798 version. This careful revision greatly enriched the poem, which remains one of the finest examples in our literature of poetic imagination combined with supreme craftsmanship in words.

6

Keats's most ambitious poetic undertaking was *Hyperion*, which he began in the autumn of the year 1818. The subject had been long in his mind, but due to many anxieties he worked at it by fits and starts then, and throughout the early part of the following year. In September 1819, he wrote to his friend Reynolds giving his reasons for discontinuing the poem as follows:

'There were too many Miltonic inversions in it—Miltonic verse cannot be written but in an artful, or rather, artist's humour. I wish to give myself up to other sensations. English ought to be kept up.'

Here is a passage from the poem:

> Meanwhile in other realms big tears were shed,
> More sorrow like to this, and such like woe,
> Too huge for mortal tongue or pen of scribe:
> The Titans fierce, self-hid, or prison-bound,
> Groan'd for the old allegiance once more,
> And listen'd in sharp pain for Saturn's voice.
> But one of the whole mammoth-brood still kept
> His sov'reignty, and rule, and majesty;—

Blazing Hyperion on his orbed fire
Still sat, still snuff'd the incense, teeming up
From man to the sun's God; yet unsecure:
For as among us mortals omens drear
Fright and perplex, so also shuddered he—
Not at dog's howl, or gloom-bird's hated screech,
Or the familiar visiting of one
Upon the first toll of his passing-bell,
Or prophesyings of the midnight lamp;
But horrors, portion'd to a giant nerve,
Oft made Hyperion ache. His palace bright
Bastion'd with pyramids of glowing gold,
And touch'd with shade of bronzed obelisks,
Glar'd a blood-red through all its thousand courts,
Arches, and domes, and fiery galleries;
And all its curtains of Aurorian clouds
Flush'd angerly: while sometimes eagle's wings,
Unseen before by Gods or wondering men,
Darken'd the place; and neighing steeds were heard,
Not heard before by Gods or wondering men.
Also, when he would taste the spicy wreaths
Of incense, breath'd aloft from sacred hills,
Instead of sweets, his ample palate took
Savour of poisonous brass and metal sick.

In November and December of 1819 Keats made an attempt to reconstruct the poem, calling it *The Fall of Hyperion*. We know that he considered the diction of *Hyperion* laboured and artificial. However, as many of the changes he made were unhappily for the worse, it was thought for many years that *The Fall of Hyperion* was in fact the first version of the poem. Internal evidence has shown conclusively that *The Fall of Hyperion* was not a first draft but a recast attempted by the poet because he was dissatisfied with the poem as it stood. The relation of the two poems is of vital interest in the study of Keats's poetic art. It is profitable to consider parallel passages side by side, and to find reasons for the omissions and alterations made in revising the piece. The former passage appears as follows in *The Fall of Hyperion*:

In melancholy realms big tears are shed,
More sorrow like to this, and such like woe,
Too huge for mortal tongue, or pen of scribe.
The Titans fierce, self hid or prison bound,
Groan for the old allegiance once more,
Listening in their doom for Saturn's voice.
But one of our whole eagle-brood still keeps
His sov'reignty, and rule, and majesty;
Blazing Hyperion on his orbed fire
Still sits, still snuffs the incense teeming up
From Man to the Sun's God: yet unsecure.
For as upon the earth dire prodigies
Fright and perplex, so also shudders he:
Nor at dog's howl or gloom-bird's Even screech,
Or the familiar visitings of one
Upon the first toll of his passing bell:
But horrors, portioned to a giant nerve,
Make great Hyperion ache. His palace bright,
Bastion'd with pyramids of glowing gold,
And touch'd with shade of bronzed obelisks,
Glares a blood-red thro' all the thousand courts,
Arches, and domes, and fiery galleries:
And all its curtains of Aurorian clouds
Flush angerly; when he would taste the wreaths
Of incense breathed aloft from sacred hills,
Instead of sweets, his ample palate takes
Savour of poisonous brass and metals sick.

7

In 1833 Tennyson published a volume of poems which included
The Lotos-Eaters. It was reviewed by Lockhart in the *Quarterly*
Review, April 1833. He did not spare the poet, hailing him as
'another and a brighter star of that galaxy or *milky way* of poetry of
which the lamented Keats was the harbinger...'. He quotes some
fourteen lines from the concluding passage of *The Lotos-Eaters*, and

says, 'Our readers will, we think, agree that this is admirably charac-
teristic, and that the singers of this song must have made pretty free
with the intoxicating fruit. How they got home you must read in
Homer: Mr Tennyson—himself, we presume, a dreamy lotus-eater,
a delicious lotus-eater—leaves them in full song.'

Here is the passage in the original version of 1833 which produced
this comment:

The Lotos-Eaters

We have had enough of motion,
Weariness and wild alarm,
Tossing on the tossing ocean,
Where the tusked sea-horse walloweth
In a stripe of grass-green calm,
At noon tide beneath the lee;
And the monstrous narwhale swalloweth
His foam-fountains in the sea.
Long enough the wine-dark wave our weary bark did carry.
This is lovelier and sweeter,
Men of Ithaca, this is meeter,
In the hollow rosy vale to tarry,
Like a dreamy Lotos-eater, a delirious Lotos-eater!
We will eat the Lotos, sweet
As the yellow honeycomb,
In the valley some, and some
On the ancient heights divine;
And no more roam,
On the loud hoar foam,
To the melancholy home
At the limit of the brine,
The little isle of Ithaca, beneath the day's decline.
We'll lift no more the shattered oar,
No more unfurl the straining sail;
With the blissful Lotos-eaters pale
We will abide in the golden vale
Of the Lotos-land till the Lotos fail;
We will not wander more.
Hark! how sweet the horned ewes bleat
On the solitary steeps,

73

And the merry lizard leaps,
And the foam-white waters pour;
And the dark pine weeps,
And the lithe vine creeps,
And the heavy melon sleeps
On the level of the shore:
Oh! islanders of Ithaca, we will not wander more.
Surely, surely slumber is more sweet than toil, the shore
Than labour in the ocean, and rowing with the oar,
Oh! islanders of Ithaca, we will return no more.

It is significant that almost every line with which the critic found fault was either omitted or re-written in future editions of Tennyson's works. Lockhart's pleasantries were certainly justified in regard to *The Lotos-Eaters*. The last part of the Choric Song was considerably altered, and Tennyson produced some of his happiest revisions. Here is the version of 1853 for purposes of comparison:

The Lotos blooms below the barren peak:
The Lotos blows by every winding creek:
All day the wind breathes low with mellower tone:
Thro' every hollow cave and alley lone
Round and round the spicy downs the yellow Lotos-dust is blown.
We have had enough of action, and of motion we,
Roll'd to starboard, roll'd to larboard, when the surge was seething
    free,
Where the wallowing monster spouted his foam-fountains in the sea.
Let us swear an oath, and keep it with an equal mind,
In the hollow Lotos-land to live and lie reclined
On the hills like Gods together, careless of mankind.
For they lie beside their nectar, and the bolts are hurl'd
Far below them in the valleys, and the clouds are lightly curl'd
Round their golden houses, girdled with the gleaming world:
Where they smile in secret, looking over wasted lands,
Blight and famine, plague and earthquake, roaring deeps and fiery
    sands,
Clanging fights, and flaming towns, and sinking ships, and praying
    hands.

74

But they smile, they find a music centred in a doleful song
Steaming up, a lamentation and an ancient tale of wrong,
Like a tale of little meaning tho' the words are strong;
Chanted from an ill-used race of men that cleave the soil,
Sow the seed, and reap the harvest with enduring toil,
Storing yearly little dues of wheat, and wine and oil;
Till they perish and they suffer—some, 'tis whisper'd—down in hell
Suffer endless anguish, others in Elysian valleys dwell,
Resting weary limbs at last on beds of asphodel.
Surely, surely, slumber is more sweet than toil, the shore
Than labour in the deep mid-ocean, wind and wave and oar;
Oh rest ye, brother mariners, we will not wander more.

8

Rossetti's *The Blessed Damozel* provides another interesting illustration of the way in which a poem may be composed only after much 'labour of the file'. This intensely individual lyric was written when the poet was nineteen years of age. It was first published in the Pre-Raphaelite periodical *The Germ*, in 1850. The poem was frequently revised in the effort to attain that perfect expression which was Rossetti's constant aim.

The final version of the poem is generally accepted as that of 1870. These lines in the first stanza:

> Her eyes were deeper than the depth
>   Of waters stilled at even;

were originally:

> Her blue grave eyes were deeper much
>   Than a deep water even.

and passed through an intermediate stage in the *Oxford and Cambridge Magazine*:

> Her eyes knew more of rest and shade
>   Than waters stilled at even.

75

The seventh stanza was the most altered. When first published it ran:

> Heard hardly, some of her new friends
>   Playing at holy games,
> Spake, gentle-mouthed among themselves
>   Their virginal new names
> And the souls mounting up to God
>   Went by her like thin flames.

In the *Oxford and Cambridge Magazine* this was changed:

> She scarcely heard her sweet new friends
>   Playing at holy games,
> Softly they spake among themselves
>   Their virginal chaste names
> And the souls mounting up to God
>   Went by her like thin flames.

This is how it reads in the 1870 version:

> Heard hardly, some of her new friends
>   Amid their loving games
> Spake evermore among themselves
>   Their virginal chaste names;
> And the souls mounting up to God
>   Went by her like thin flames.

Two other examples will suffice to show how this delicate, archaic, imaginative poem was fastidiously revised to its final form.

Stanza eight appears in *The Germ* as follows:

> And still she bowed herself and stooped
>   Into the vast waste calm,
> Till her bosom's pressure must have made
>   The bar she leaned on warm.
> And the lilies lay as if asleep
>   Along her bended arm.

The first four lines were revised in the *Oxford and Cambridge Magazine*:

> And still she bowed above the vast
>   Waste sea of worlds that swam,
> Until her bosom must have made
>   The bar she leaned on warm.

This is how the stanza finally appeared:

> And still she bowed herself and stooped
>   Out of the circling charm;
> Until her bosom must have made
>   The bar she leaned on warm,
> And the lilies lay as if asleep
>   Along her bended arm.

In the next stanza changes are made which once again improve the poem. In *The Germ* the stanza reads:

> From the fixt lull of heaven she saw
>   Time, like a pulse, shake fierce
> Through all the worlds. Her gaze still strove,
>   In that steep gulf, to pierce
> The swarm: and then she spake as when
>   The stars sang in their spheres.

This is its final form:

> From the fixed place of Heaven she saw
>   Time like a pulse shake fierce
> Through all the worlds. Her gaze still strove
>   Within the gulf to pierce
> Its path; and now she spoke as when
>   The stars sang in their spheres.

Rossetti spared no pains; only four verses in the whole poem remained unaltered since 1848 when it was first composed. Even in 1881 we find him hesitating between 'she *cast* her arms along the golden barriers', and 'she *laid* her arms...', and in the last four words of the poem considering whether to say 'I *heard* her tears' or 'I *felt* her tears'.

Such patient labour as this shows that he was as deliberate an artist as Herrick or Keats or Tennyson, combining fastidious workmanship and lyrical inspiration.

III

THE POET'S RAW MATERIAL

1

From Sir Thomas North's *Translation of Plutarch's 'Lives of the Noble Grecians and Romans'*.

Therefore when she was sent unto by divers letters, both from *Antonius* himself, and also from his friends, she made so light of it, and mocked *Antonius* so much, that she disdained to set forward otherwise, but to take her barge in the river of *Cydnus*; the poop whereof was of gold, the sails of purple, and the oars of silver, which kept stroke in rowing after the sound of the musicke of flutes, howboys, citherns, viols, and such other instruments as they played upon in the barge. And now for the person of herself: she was laid under a pavilion of cloth of gold of tissue, apparelled and attired like the goddess *Venus* commonly drawn in picture: and hard by her, on either hand of her, pretty fair boys apparelled as Painters do set forth god *Cupid*, with little fans in their hands, with the which they fanned wind upon her. Her Ladies and Gentlewomen also, the fairest of them were apparelled like the Nymphs *Nereids* (which are the mermaids of the waters) and like the *Graces*, some steering the helm, others tending the tackle and ropes of the barge, out of the which there came a wonderful passing sweet savour of perfumes, that perfumed the wharf's side, pestered with innumerable multitudes of people. Some of them followed the barge all along the river-side: others also ran out of the city to see her coming in. So that in the end there ran such multitudes of people one after another to see her, that *Antonius* was left post alone in the market-place in his Imperial seat to give audience: and there went a rumour in the people's mouths, that the goddess *Venus* was come to play with the god *Bacchus*, for the general good of all Asia.

From Shakespeare's *Antony and Cleopatra* (Act II, scene ii).

> The barge she sat in, like a burnish'd throne,
> Burn'd on the water: the poop was beaten gold;
> Purple the sails, and so perfumed that
> The winds were love-sick with them; the oars were silver,

6   81

Which to the tune of flutes kept stroke, and made
The water which they beat to follow faster,
As amorous of their strokes. For her own person,
It beggar'd all description: she did lie
In her pavilion—cloth-of-gold of tissue—
O'er-picturing that of Venus where we see
The fancy outwork nature: on each side her
Stood pretty dimpled boys, like smiling Cupids,
With divers-coloured fans, whose wind did seem
To glow the delicate cheeks which they did cool,
And what they undid did.

Her gentlewomen, like the Nereides,
So many mermaids, tended her i' the eyes,
And made their bends adornings: at the helm
A seeming mermaid steers: the silken tackle
Swell with the touches of those flower-soft hands,
That yarely frame the office. From the barge
A strange invisible perfume hits the sense
Of the adjacent wharfs. The city cast
Her people out upon her; and Antony,
Enthroned i' the market-place, did sit alone,
Whistling to the air; which, but for vacancy,
Had gone to gaze on Cleopatra too,
And made a gap in nature.

2

From Sir Thomas North's *Translation of Plutarch's 'Lives of the Noble Grecians and Romans'*.

The Senate being afeard of their departure, did send unto them certain of the pleasantest old men, and the most acceptable to the people among them. Of these Menenius Agrippa was he, who was sent for chief man of the message from the Senate. He, after many good persuasions and gentle requests made to the people, on the behalf of the Senate: knit up his oration in the end, with a notable tale, in this manner. That on a time all the members of man's body did rebel against the belly, complaining of it, that it only remained in the midst of the body, without doing anything, neither did bear any labour to the maintenance of the rest: whereas all other parts and members did labour painfully, and were very careful to satisfy the appetites and desires of the body. And so the belly, all this notwithstanding laughed at their folly, and said: It is true, I first receive all meats that nourish man's body; but afterwards I send it again to the nourishment of other parts of the same. Even so (quoth he) O you, my maisters, and citizens of Rome: the reason is alike between the Senate and you. For matters being well digested, and their counsels thoroughly examined, touching the benefit of the commonwealth: the Senators are cause of the common commodity that cometh unto every one of you.

From Shakespeare's *Coriolanus* (Act I, scene i).

Menenius. Either you must
Confess yourselves wondrous malicious,
Or be accus'd of folly. I shall tell you
A pretty tale: it may be you have heard it;
But, since it serves my purpose, I will venture
To stale't a little more.
    First Citizen. Well, I'll hear it, sir: yet you must not think to
fob-off our disgrace with a tale: but, an't please you deliver.
    Menenius. There was a time when all the body's members
Rebell'd against the belly; thus accus'd it:—
That only like a gulf it did remain
I' the midst o' the body, idle and unactive,
Still cupboarding the viand, never bearing
Like labour with the rest; where th'other instruments
Did see and hear, devise, instruct, walk, feel,
And, mutually participate, did minister
Unto the appetite and affection common
Of the whole body. The belly answer'd,—
    First Citizen. Well, sir, what answer made the belly?
    Menenius. Sir, I shall tell you.—With a kind of smile,
Which ne'er came from the lungs, but even thus—
For, look you, I may make the belly smile

As well as speak—it tauntingly replied
To the discontented members, the mutinous parts
That envied his receipt; even so most fitly
As you malign our senators for that
They are not such as you.
    First Citizen.   Your belly's answer? What!
The kingly-crowned head, the vigilant eye,
The counsellor heart, the arm our soldier,
Our steed the leg, the tongue our trumpeter,
With other muniments and petty helps
In this our fabric, if that they—
    Menenius.   What then?—
'Fore me, this fellow speaks!—what then? what then?
    First Citizen. Should by the cormorant belly be restrain'd,
Who is the sink o' the body,—
    Menenius.   Well, what then?
    First Citizen. The former agents, if they did complain,
What could the belly answer?
    Menenius.   I will tell you;
If you'll bestow a small—of what you have little—
Patience awhile, you'll hear the belly's answer.
    First Citizen. Y'are long about it.
    Menenius.   Note me this, good friend;
Your most grave belly was deliberate,
Not rash like his accusers, and thus answer'd:
'True is it, my incorporate friends,' quoth he,
'That I receive the general food at first,
Which you do live upon; and fit it is,
Because I am the store-house and the shop
Of the whole body: but, if you do remember,
I send it through the rivers of your blood,
Even to the court, the heart,—to the seat o' the brain;
And, through the cranks and offices of man,
The strongest nerves and small inferior veins
From me receive that natural competency
Whereby they live: and though that all at once,
You, my good friends,'—this says the belly, mark me,—
    First Citizen. Ay, sir; well, well.
    Menenius.   'Though all at once can not

84

See what I do deliver out to each,
Yet I can make my audit up, that all
From me do back receive the flour of all
And leave me but the bran.'—What say you to't?
   First Citizen. It was an answer: how apply you this?
   Menenius. The senators of Rome are this good belly,
And you the mutinous members: for examine
Their counsels and their cares; digest things rightly
Touching the weal o' the common; you shall find,
No public benefit which you receive
But it proceeds or comes from them to you,
And no way from yourselves.

3

From Arthur Golding's *Translation of Ovid's 'Metamorphoses'* VII.

Ye Airs and Winds: ye Elves of Hills, of Brooks, of Woods alone,
Of standing Lakes, and of the Night approach ye everyone.
Through help of whom (the crooked banks much wondering at the
    thing)
I have compelled streams to run clean backward to their spring.
By charms I make the calm seas rough, and make the rough seas
    plain.
And cover all the sky with clouds and chase them hence again.
By charms I raise and lay the winds, and burst the Vipers jaw.
And from the bowels of the earth both stones and trees do draw.
Whole Woods and Forests I remove: I make the mountains shake,
And even the earth itself to groan and fearfully to quake.
I call up dead men from their graves and thee, O lightsome Moon
I darken oft, though beaten brass abate thy peril soon.
Our Sorcery dims the Morning fair, and darks the Sun at noon.

From Shakespeare's *The Tempest* (Act v, scene i).

    Ye elves of hills, brooks, standing lakes, and groves,
    And ye that on the sands with printless foot
    Do chase the ebbing Neptune, and do fly him
    When he comes back; you demi-puppets that

By moonshine do the green sour ringlets make,
Whereof the ewe not bites; and you whose pastime
Is to make midnight mushrooms, that rejoice
To hear the solemn curfew; by whose aid—
Weak masters though ye be—I have bedimm'd
The noontide sun, call'd forth the mutinous winds,
And 'twixt the green sea and the azur'd vault
Set roaring war: to the dread rattling thunder
Have I given fire, and rifted Jove's stout oak
With his own bolt; the strong-bas'd promontory
Have I made shake, and by the spurs pluck'd up
The pine and cedar; graves at my command
Have wak'd their sleepers, op'd, and let them forth
By my so potent art.

4

From Holinshed's *Chronicles*.

For the space of six months together, after this heinous murder thus committed, there appeared no sun by day nor moon by night in any part of the realm, but still was the sky covered with continual clouds, and sometimes such outrageous winds arose, with lightnings and tempests, that the people were in great fear of present destruction....

Monstrous sights also that were seen within the Scottish kingdom that year were these: horses in Lothian, being of singular beauty and swiftness, did eat their own flesh, and would in no wise taste any other meat. There was a sparrowhawk also strangled by an owl. Neither was it any less wonder that the sun, as before is said, was continually covered with clouds for six months space. But all men understood that the abominable murder of King Duffe was the cause hereof.

From Shakespeare's *Macbeth* (Act II, scene iv).

Old Man. Threescore and ten I can remember well:
Within the volume of which time I have seen

Hours dreadful and things strange; but this sore night
Hath trifled former knowings.
    Ross.   Ha, good father,
Thou seest, the heavens, as troubled with man's act,
Threatens his bloody stage: by th' clock 'tis day,
And yet dark night strangles the travelling lamp:
Is't night's predominance, or the day's shame,
That darkness does the face of earth entomb,
When living light should kiss it?
    Old Man.   'Tis unnatural,
Even like the deed that's done. On Tuesday last,
A falcon, towering in her pride of place,
Was by a mousing owl hawk'd at and kill'd.
    Ross. And Duncan's horses—a thing most strange and certain,—
Beauteous and swift, the minions of their race,
Turn'd wild in nature, broke their stalls, flung out,
Contending 'gainst obedience, as they would make
War with mankind.
    Old Man.   'Tis said they eat each other.
    Ross. They did so,—to th' amazement of mine eyes,
That look'd upon 't.

5

From the *Decameron* of Boccaccio, the Fifth Story on the Fourth
Day.

And so, saddest of women, knowing that she might not bewail him
there, she would gladly, if she could, have carried away the body
and given it more honourable sepulture elsewhere; but as she might
not do so, she took a knife, and, as best she could, severed the head
from the trunk, and wrapped it in a napkin and laid it in the lap of
her maid; and having covered the rest of the corpse with earth, she
left the spot, having been seen by none, and went home. There she
shut herself up in her room with the head, and kissed it a thousand
times in every part, and wept long and bitterly over it, till she had

bathed it in her tears. She then wrapped it in a piece of fine cloth, and set it in a large and beautiful pot of the sort in which marjoram or basil is planted, and covered it with earth, and therein planted some roots of the goodliest basil of Salerno, and drenched them only with her tears, or water perfumed with roses or orange-blossoms. And 'twas her wont ever to sit beside this pot, and, all her soul one yearning, to pore upon it, as that which enshrined her Lorenzo, and when long time she had so done, she would bend over it, and weep a great while, until the basil was quite bathed in her tears.

Fostered with such constant, unremitting care, and nourished by the richness given to the soil by the decaying head that lay therein, the basil burgeoned out in exceeding great beauty and fragrance. And, the girl persevering ever in this way of life, the neighbours from time to time took note of it, and when her brothers marvelled to see her beauty ruined, and her eyes as it were evanished from her head, they told them of it, saying: 'We have observed that such is her daily wont.'

From Keats's *Isabella; or, The Pot of Basil.*

L

With duller steel than the Persean sword
They cut away no formless monster's head,
But one, whose gentleness did well accord
With death, as life. The ancient harps have said,
Love never dies, but lives, immortal Lord:
If Love impersonate was ever dead,
Pale Isabella kiss'd it, and low moan'd.
'Twas love; cold,—dead indeed, but not dethroned.

LI

In anxious secrecy they took it home,
And then the prize was all to Isabel:
She calm'd its wild hair with a golden comb,
And all around each eye's sepulchral cell
Pointed each fringed lash; the smeared loam
With tears, as chilly as a dripping well,
She drench'd away:—and still she comb'd, and kept
Sighing all day—and still she kiss'd, and wept.

LII

Then in a silken scarf,—sweet with the dews
Of precious flowers pluck'd in Araby,
And divine liquids come with odorous ooze
Through the cold serpent-pipe refreshfully,—
She wrapped it up; and for its tomb did choose
A garden-pot, wherein she laid it by,
And cover'd it with mould, and o'er it set
Sweet Basil, which her tears kept ever wet.

LIII

And she forgot the stars, the moon, and sun,
And she forgot the blue above the trees,
And she forgot the dells where waters run,
And she forgot the chilly autumn breeze;
She had no knowledge when the day was done,
And the new morn she saw not: but in peace
Hung over her sweet Basil evermore,
And moisten'd it with tears unto the core.

LIV

And so she ever fed it with thin tears,
Whence thick, and green, and beautiful it grew,
So that it smelt more balmy than its peers
Of Basil-tufts in Florence; for it drew
Nurture besides, and life, from human fears,
From the fast mouldering head there shut from view:
So that the jewel safely casketed,
Came forth, and in perfumed leafits spread.

* * * * *

LVIII

And, furthermore, her brethren wonder'd much
Why she sat drooping by the Basil green;
And why it flourish'd, as by magic touch;
Greatly they wonder'd what the thing might mean:
They could not surely give belief, that such
A very nothing would have power to wean
Her from her own fair youth, and pleasures gay,
And even remembrance of her love's delay.

6

Tennyson went to Sir Thomas Malory's *Le Morte d'Arthur* for his blank verse *Morte D'Arthur*. It is interesting to compare the two. Here is an extract from *Le Morte d'Arthur* as printed by Caxton in 1485, but with the spelling modernized, and with the addition of quotation marks and paragraphing.

'Therefore,' said Arthur unto Sir Bedivere, 'take thou Excalibur my good sword, and go with it to yonder water side, and when thou comest there I charge thee throw my sword in that water, and come again and tell me what thou there seest.'

'My lord,' said Bedivere, 'your commandment shall be done, and lightly bring you word again.'

So Sir Bedivere departed, and by the way he beheld that noble sword, that the pommel and the haft was all of precious stones; and then he said to himself: 'If I throw this rich sword in the water, thereof shall never come good, but harm and loss.' And then Sir Bedivere hid Excalibur under a tree.

And so, as soon as he might, he came again unto the king, and said he had been at the water, and had thrown the sword in the water.

'What saw thou there?' said the king.

'Sir,' he said, 'I saw nothing but waves and winds.'

'That is untruly said of thee,' said the king, 'therefore go thou lightly again, and do my commandment; as thou art to me lief and dear, spare not but throw it in.'

Then Sir Bedivere returned again, and took the sword in his hand: and then him thought sin and shame to throw away that noble sword, and so efte he hid the sword, and returned again, and told to the king that he had been at the water, and done his commandment.

'What saw thou there?' said the king.

'Sir,' he said, 'I saw nothing but the waters wappe and waves wanne.'

'Ah, traitor untrue,' said King Arthur, 'now hast thou betrayed me twice. Who would have weened that, thou that hast been to me so lief and dear? and thou art named a noble knight, and would betray me for the richness of the sword. But now go again lightly, for thy long tarrying putteth me in great jeopardy of my life, for I have taken cold. And but if thou do now as I bid thee, if ever I may see thee, I shall slay thee with mine own hands; for thou wouldst for my rich sword see me dead.'

Then Sir Bedivere departed, and went to the sword, and lightly took it up, and went to the water side; and there he bound the girdle about the hilts, and then he threw the sword as far into the water as he might; and there came an arm and an hand above the water and met it, and caught it, and so shook it thrice and brandished, and then vanished away the hand with the sword in the water.

So Sir Bedivere came again to the king, and told him what he saw. 'Alas,' said the king, 'help me hence, for I dread me I have tarried over long.'

Then Sir Bedivere took the king upon his back, and so went with him to that water side. And when they were at the water side, even fast by the bank hoved a little barge with many fair ladies in it, and among them all was a queen, and all they had black hoods, and all they wept and shrieked when they saw King Arthur.

'Now put me into the barge', said the king.

And so he did softly. And there received him three queens with great mourning; and so they set them down, and in one of their laps King Arthur laid his head.

And then that queen said: 'Ah, dear brother, why have ye tarried so long from me? alas, this wound on your head hath caught overmuch cold.'

And so then they rowed from the land, and Sir Bedivere beheld all those ladies go from him.

Then Sir Bedivere cried: 'Ah, my lord Arthur, what shall become of me, now ye go from me and leave me here alone among mine enemies?'

'Comfort thyself,' said the king, 'and do as well as thou mayest, for in me is no trust for to trust in. For I will into the vale of Avilion to heal me of my grievous wound: and if thou hear nevermore of me, pray for my soul.'

But ever the queens and ladies wept and shrieked, that it was pity to hear. And as soon as Sir Bedivere had lost the sight of the barge, he wept and wailed, and so took the forest.

Tennyson's *Morte D'Arthur* was published in 1842 and subsequently incorporated in *The Passing of Arthur*, one of the *Idylls of*
the King.

Then spake King Arthur to Sir Bedivere:
'Thou therefore take my brand Excalibur,
Which was my pride: for thou rememberest how
In those old days, one summer noon, an arm
Rose up from out the bosom of the lake,
Clothed in white samite, mystic, wonderful,
Holding the sword—and how I row'd across
And took it, and have worn it, like a king:
And wheresoever I am sung or told
In aftertime, this also shall be known:
But now delay not: take Excalibur,
And fling him far into the middle mere:
Watch what thou seest, and lightly bring me word.'
    To him replied the bold Sir Bedivere:
'It is not meet, Sir King, to leave thee thus,
Aidless, alone, and smitten thro' the helm
A little thing may harm a wounded man.
Yet I thy hest will all perform at full,
Watch what I see, and lightly bring thee word.'
    So saying, from the ruin'd shrine he stept
And in the moon athwart the place of tombs,
Where lay the mighty bones of ancient men,
Old knights, and over them the sea-wind sang
Shrill, chill, with flakes of foam. He, stepping down
By zig-zag paths, and juts of pointed rock,
Came on the shining levels of the lake.
    There drew he forth the brand Excalibur,
And o'er him drawing it, the winter moon,
Brightening the skirts of a long cloud, ran forth
And sparkled keen with frost against the hilt:
For all the haft twinkled with diamond studs
Myriads of topaz-lights, and jacinth-work
Of subtlest jewellery. He gazed so long
That both his eyes were dazzled, as he stood,
This way and that dividing the swift mind,

In act to throw: but at the last it seem'd
Better to leave Excalibur conceal'd
There in the many-knotted waterflags,
That whistled stiff and dry about the marge.
So strode he back slow to the wounded king.

   Then spake King Arthur to Sir Bedivere:
'Hast thou perform'd my mission which I gave?
What is it thou hast seen? or what hast heard?'

   And answer made the bold Sir Bedivere:
'I heard the ripple washing in the reeds,
And the wild water lapping on the crag.'

   To whom replied King Arthur, faint and pale:
'Thou hast betrayed thy nature and thy name,
Not rendering true answer, as beseem'd
Thy fealty, not like a noble knight:
For surer sign had followed, either hand,
Or voice, or else a motion of the mere.
This is a shameful thing for men to lie.
Yet now, I charge thee, quickly go again
As thou art lief and dear, and do the thing
I bad thee, watch, and lightly bring me word.'

   Then went Sir Bedivere the second time
Across the ridge, and paced beside the mere,
Counting the dewy pebbles, fix'd in thought;
But when he saw the wonder of the hilt,
How curiously and strangely chased, he smote
His palms together, and he cried aloud.

   'And if indeed I cast the brand away,
Surely a precious thing, one worthy note,
Should thus be lost for ever from the earth
Which might have pleased the eyes of many men.'
What good should follow this, if this were done?
What harm, undone? deep harm to disobey,
Seeing obedience is the bond of rule.
Were it well to obey then, if a king demand
An act unprofitable, against himself?
The King is sick, and knows not what he does.
What record, or what relic of my lord
Should be to aftertime, but empty breath

And rumours of a doubt? but were this kept,
Stored in some treasure-house of mighty kings,
Some one might show it at a joust of arms,
Saying, "King Arthur's sword, Excalibur,
Wrought by the lonely maiden of the Lake.
Nine years she wrought it, sitting in the deeps
Upon the hidden bases of the hills."
So might some old man speak in the aftertime
To all the people, winning reverence.
But now much honour and much fame were lost.'
   So spake he, clouded with his own conceit,
And hid Excalibur the second time,
And so strode back slow to the wounded King.
   Then spoke King Arthur, breathing heavily:
'What is it thou hast seen? or what hast heard?'
   And answer made the bold Sir Bedivere:
'I heard the water lapping on the crag,
And the long ripple washing in the reeds.'
   To whom replied King Arthur, much in wrath:
'Ah, miserable and unkind, untrue,
Unknightly, traitor-hearted! Woe is me!
Authority forgets a dying king,
Laid widow'd of the power in his eye
That bow'd the will. I see thee what thou art,
For thou, the latest-left of all my knights,
In whom should meet the offices of all,
Thou wouldst betray me for the precious hilt;
Either from lust of gold, or like a girl
Valuing the giddy pleasure of the eyes.
Yet, for a man may fail in duty twice,
And the third time may prosper, get thee hence:
But, if thou spare to fling Excalibur,
I will arise and slay thee with my hands.'
   Then quickly rose Sir Bedivere, and ran,
And, leaping down the ridges lightly, plunged
Among the bulrush-beds, and clutch'd the sword,
And strongly wheel'd and threw it. The great brand
Made lightnings in the splendour of the moon,
And flashing round and round, and whirl'd in an arch,

Shot like a streamer of the northern morn,
Seen where the moving isles of winter shock
By night, with noises of the northern sea.
So flash'd and fell the brand Excalibur:
But ere he dipt the surface, rose an arm
Clothed in white samite, mystic, wonderful,
And caught him by the hilt, and brandish'd him
Three times, and drew him under in the mere.
And lightly went the other to the King.
Then spoke King Arthur, drawing thicker breath:
'Now see I by thine eyes that this is done.
Speak out: what is it thou hast heard, or seen?'
  And answer made the bold Sir Bedivere:
'Sir King, I closed mine eyelids, lest the gems
Should blind my purpose, for I never saw,
Nor shall see, here or elsewhere, till I die,
Not tho' I live three lives of mortal men,
So great a miracle as yonder hilt.
Then with both hands I flung him, wheeling him;
But when I look'd again, behold an arm,
Clothed in white samite, mystic, wonderful,
That caught him by the hilt, and brandish'd him
Three times, and drew him under in the mere.'
  And answer made King Arthur, breathing hard:
'My end draws nigh; 'tis time that I were gone.
Make broad thy shoulders to receive my weight,
And bear me to the margin; yet I fear
My wound hath taken cold, and I shall die.'
  So saying, from the pavement he half rose,
Slowly, with pain, reclining on his arm,
And looking wistfully with wide blue eyes
As in a picture. Him Sir Bedivere
Remorsefully regarded thro' his tears,
And would have spoken, but he found not words,
Then took with care, and kneeling on one knee
O'er both his shoulders drew the languid hands,
And rising bore him thro' the place of tombs.
  But as he walk'd, King Arthur panted hard,
Like one that feels a nightmare on his bed

When all the house is mute. So sigh'd the King,
Muttering and murmuring at his ear 'Quick, quick!
I fear it is too late, and I shall die.'
But the other swiftly strode from ridge to ridge,
Clothed with his breath, and looking as he walk'd,
Larger than human on the frozen hills.
He heard the deep behind him, and a cry
Before. His own thought drove him like a goad.
Dry clash'd his harness in the icy caves
And barren chasms, and all to left and right
The bare black cliff clang'd round him, as he based
His feet on juts of slippery crag that rang
Sharp-smitten with the dint of armed heels—
And on a sudden, lo! the level lake,
And the long glories of the winter moon.

   Then saw they how there hove a dusky barge,
Dark as a funeral scarf from stem to stern,
Beneath them; and descending they were ware
That all the decks were dense with stately forms
Black-stoled, black-hooded, like a dream—by these
Three Queens with crowns of gold—and from them rose
A cry that shiver'd to the tingling stars,
And, as it were one voice, an agony
Of lamentation, like a wind, that shrills
All night in a waste land, where no one comes,
Or hath come, since the making of the world.

   Then murmur'd Arthur, 'Place me in the barge',
And to the barge they came. There those three Queens
Put forth their hands, and took the King, and wept.
But she, that rose the tallest of them all
And fairest, laid his head upon her lap,
And loosed the shatter'd casque, and chafed his hands,
And call'd him by his name, complaining loud,
And dropping bitter tears against his brow
Striped with dark blood: for all his face was white
And colourless, and like the wither'd moon
Smote by the fresh beam of the springing east;
And all his greaves and cuisses dash'd with drops
Of onset; and the light and lustrous curls—

96

That made his forehead like a rising sun
High from the dais-throne—were parch'd with dust;
Or, clotted into points and hanging loose,
Mix'd with the knightly growth that fringed his lips.
So like a shatter'd column lay the King;
Not like that Arthur who, with lance in rest,
From spur to plume a star of tournament,
Shot thro' the lists at Camelot, and charged
Before the eyes of ladies and of kings.

   Then loudly cried the bold Sir Bedivere,
'Ah! my Lord Arthur, whither shall I go?
Where shall I hide my forehead and my eyes?
For now I see the true old times are dead,
When every morning brought a noble chance,
And every chance brought out a noble knight.
Such times have been not since the light that led
The holy Elders with the gift of myrrh.
But now the whole ROUND TABLE is dissolved
Which was an image of the mighty world;
And I, the last, go forth companionless,
And the days darken round me, and the years,
Among new men, strange faces, other minds.'

   And slowly answer'd Arthur from the barge:
'The old order changeth, yielding place to new,
And God fulfils himself in many ways,
Lest one good custom should corrupt the world.
Comfort thyself: what comfort is in me?
I have lived my life, and that which I have done
May He within himself make pure! but thou,
If thou shouldst never see my face again,
Pray for my soul. More things are wrought by prayer
Than this world dreams of. Whereof, let thy voice
Rise like a fountain for me night and day.
For what are men better than sheep or goats
That nourish a blind life within the brain,
If, knowing God, they lift not hands of prayer
Both for themselves and those who call them friend?
For so the whole round earth is every way
Bound by gold chains about the feet of God.

But now farewell. I am going a long way
With these thou seest—if indeed I go—
(For all my mind is clouded with a doubt)
To the island-valley of Avilion;
Where falls not hail, or rain, or any snow,
Nor ever wind blows loudly; but it lies
Deep-meadow'd, happy, fair with orchard-lawns
And bowery hollows crown'd with summer sea,
Where I will heal me of my grievous wound.'
  So said he, and the barge with oar and sail
Moved from the brink, like some full-breasted swan
That, fluting a wild carol ere her death,
Ruffles her pure cold plume, and takes the flood
With swarthy webs. Long stood Sir Bedivere
Revolving many memories, till the hull
Look'd one black dot against the verge of dawn,
And on the mere the wailing died away.

IV

THE POET'S TRANSLATION

HOMER

Iliad VIII, 542–61

(a)

This speech all Trojans did applaud; who from their traces los'd
Their sweating horse, which sev'rally with headstalls they repos'd,
And fast'ned by their chariots; when others brought from town
Fat sheep and oxen, instantly, bread, wine, and hewéd down
Huge store of wood. The winds transferr'd into the friendly sky
Their supper's savour; to the which they sat delightfully,
And spent all night in open field; fires round about them shin'd.
As when about the silver moon, when air is free from wind,
And stars shine clear, to whose sweet beams, high prospects, and
    the brows
Of all steep hills and pinnacles, thrust up themselves for shows,
And ev'n the lowly valleys joy to glitter in their sight,
When the unmeasur'd firmament bursts to disclose her light,
And all the signs in heav'n are seen, that glad the shepherd's heart;
So many fires disclos'd their beams, made by the Trojan part,
Before the face of Ilion, and her bright turrets show'd.
A thousand courts of guard kept fires, and ev'ry guard allow'd
Fifty stout men, by whom their horse ate oats and hard white corn,
And all did wishfully expect the silver-thronéd morn.

GEORGE CHAPMAN, 1611

(b)

The leader spoke. From all his host around
Shouts of applause along the shores resound.
Each from the yoke the smoking steeds untied,
And fix'd their headstalls to his chariot-side.
Fat sheep and oxen from the town are led,
With generous wine, and all-sustaining bread.
Full hecatombs lay burning on the shore;
The winds to heaven the curling vapours bore.
Ungrateful offering to th'immortal powers!

Whose wrath hung heavy o'er the Trojan towers;
Nor Priam nor his sons obtained their grace;
Proud Troy they hated, and her guilty race.
    The troops exulting sat in order round,
And beaming fires illumined all the ground.
As when the moon, refulgent lamp of night,
O'er heaven's clear azure spreads her sacred light,
When not a breath disturbs the deep serene,
And not a cloud o'ercasts the solemn scene;
Around her throne the vivid planets roll,
And stars unnumber'd gild the glowing pole,
O'er the dark trees a yellower verdure shed,
And tip with silver every mountain's head;
Then shine the vales, the rocks in prospect rise,
A flood of glory bursts from all the skies:
The conscious swains, rejoicing in the sight,
Eye the blue vault, and bless the useful light.
So many flames before proud Ilion blaze,
And lighten glimmering Xanthus with their rays:
The long reflections of the distant fires
Gleam on the walls, and tremble on the spires.
A thousand piles the dusky horrors gild,
And shoot a shady lustre o'er the field.
Full fifty guards each flaming pile attend,
Whose umber'd arms, by fits, thick flashes send.
Loud neigh the coursers o'er their heaps of corn,
And ardent warriors wait the rising morn.

ALEXANDER POPE, 1715

(c)

Thus Hector spoke; the Trojans shouted loud:
Then from the yoke the sweating steeds they loosed,
And tethered each beside their several cars:
Next from the city speedily they brought
Oxen and sheep; the luscious wine procured;
Brought bread from out their houses, and good store
Of fuel gathered; wafted from the plain,
The winds to Heaven the savoury odours bore.

Full of proud hopes, upon the pass of war,
All night they camped, and frequent blazed their fires.
As when in Heaven, around the glittering moon
The stars shine bright amid the breathless air;
And every crag and every jutting peak
Stands boldly forth, and every forest glade;
Even to the gates of Heaven is opened wide
The boundless sky; shines each particular star
Distinct; joy fills the gazing shepherd's heart.
So bright, so thickly scattered o'er the plain,
Before the walls of Troy, between the ships
And Xanthus' stream, the Trojan watchfires blazed.
A thousand fires burnt brightly; and round each
Sat fifty warriors in the ruddy glare;
Champing the provender before them laid,
Barley and rye, the tethered horses stood
Beside the cars, and waited for the morn.

LORD DERBY, 1864

(d)

So Hector spoke; the Trojans roared applause,
Then loosed their sweating horses from the yoke,
And each beside his chariot bound his own;
And oxen from the city, and goodly sheep
In haste they drove, and honey-hearted wine
And bread from out the houses brought, and heaped
Their firewood, and the winds from off the plain
Rolled the rich vapour far into the heaven.
And these all night upon the bridge of war
Sat glorying; many a fire before them blazed:
As when in heaven the stars about the moon
Look beautiful, when all the winds are laid,
And every height comes out, and jutting peak
And valley, and the immeasurable heavens
Break open to their highest, and all the stars
Shine, and the shepherd gladdens in his heart:
So many a fire between the ships and stream
Of Xanthus blazed before the towers of Troy,

A thousand on the plain; and close by each
Sat fifty in the blaze of burning fire;
And eating hoary grain and pulse the steeds,
Fixt by their cars, waited the golden dawn.

LORD TENNYSON, 1868

HOMER

Odyssey XXIV, 1–14

(*a*)

Cyllenian Hermes, with his golden rod,
The Wooers' souls, that yet retain'd abode
Amidst their bodies, call'd in dreadful rout
Forth to th' Infernals; who came murmuring out.
And as amidst the desolate retreat
Of some vast cavern, made the sacred seat
Of austere spirits, bats with breasts and wings
Clasp fast the walls, and each to other clings,
But, swept off from their coverts, up they rise
And fly with murmurs in amazeful guise
About the cavern; so these, grumbling, rose
And flock'd together. Down before them goes
None-hurting Mercury to Hell's broad ways,
And straight to those straits, where the ocean stays
His lofty current in calm deeps, they flew.
Then to the snowy rock they next withdrew,
And to the close of Phoebus' orient gates.
The nation then of dreams, and then the states
Of those souls' idols that the weary dead
Gave up in earth, which in a flow'ry mead
Had habitable situatión.

GEORGE CHAPMAN, 1615

(*b*)

And now Cyllenian Hermes summon'd forth
The spirits of the suitors; waving wide
The golden wand of power to seal all eyes

104

In slumber, and to ope them wide again,
He drove them gibbering down into the shades.
As when the bats within some hallow'd cave
Flit squeaking all around, for if but one
Fall from the rock, the rest all follow him,
In such connexion mutual they adhere;
So, after bounteous Mercury, the ghosts
Troop'd downward gibbering all the dreary way.
The Ocean's flood and the Leucadian rock,
The Sun's gate also and the land of Dreams
They pass'd, whence next into the meads they came
Of Asphodel, by shadowy forms possess'd,
Simulars of the dead.

WILLIAM COWPER, 1791

(*c*)

But now the ghosts of the men who were of the wooers' band
Called forth Cyllenian Hermes; and he had his staff in hand,
Lovely and golden, wherewith he lulleth the eyes of men,
Whomsoever he willeth, while others from slumber he rouseth
 again.
Therewith he roused and drave them, who gibbering went along;
As when in the inmost ingle of a wondrous den the throng
Of night-bats gibbereth fluttering, when one falleth off aloof
From their chain, where clustered together they hang from the
 rocky roof,
So fared their flock a-twittering, and Hermes void of wrong
Adown the dusky highway led all the band along:
There by the streams of Ocean and the White Rock went their band,
By the gates of the Sun they wended and by the dream-folk's land,
Till in no long while they were gotten to the meads of asphodel,
Wherein the ghosts, the pictures of outworn men-folk, dwell.

WILLIAM MORRIS, 1887

(*d*)

Now Hermes of Cyllene called to the world beyond
The wraiths of the fallen Suitors—in hand he bore his wand,
Fair-wrought in gold, wherewith he charms the eyes of men
To sleep, and out of slumber awakens them again.

With it he roused the Suitors, and led them—shrieking shrill
They followed; as squeaking flutter the hosts of bats that fill
The nooks of some great grotto if one shall chance to fall
From the chain that clusters clinging to the cavern's rocky wall.
So, gibbering, on Hermes the Saviour in his flight
They followed, where he led them on the mouldering paths of night—
Past the great gateway of the Sun, past Ocean's streams,
Past the White Rock they hastened, and past the Land of Dreams,
Until at the last they came to the Meadow of Asphodel,
Where the phantoms of the weary, the souls of the perished dwell....

F. L. LUCAS, 1948

HOMERIC HYMN

To the Earth

(*a*)

Mother of all things, the well-founded Earth,
My Muse shall memorize; who all the birth
Gives food that all her upper regions breed,
All that in her divine diffusions feed
In under continents, all those that live
In all the seas, and all the air doth give
Wing'd expeditions, of thy bounties eat;
Fair children, and fair fruits, thy labour's sweat,
O great in reverence; and referr'd to thee,
For life and death is all the pedigree
Of mortal humans. Happy then is he
Whom the innate propensions of thy mind
Stand bent to honour. He shall all things find
In all abundance; all his pastures yield
Herds in all plenties; all his roofs are fill'd
With rich possessions; he, in all the sway
Of laws best order'd, cuts out his own way
In cities shining with delicious dames,
And takes his choice of all those striving flames;
High happiness and riches, like his train,
Follow his fortunes, with delights that reign

In all their princes; glory invests his sons;
His daughters, with their crown'd selections
Of all the city, frolic through the meads,
And every one her call'd-for dances treads
Along the soft-flow'r of the claver-grass.
All this, with all those, ever comes to pass,
That thy love blesses, Goddess full of grace,
And treasurous Angel t' all the human race.
  Hail, then, Great Mother of the Deified Kind,
Wife to the cope of stars! Sustain a mind
Propitious to me for my praise, and give
(Answering my mind) my vows fit means to live.

GEORGE CHAPMAN, 1616

(b)

O universal Mother, who dost keep
From everlasting thy foundations deep,
Eldest of things, Great Earth, I sing of thee!
All shapes that have their dwelling in the sea,
All things that fly, or on the ground divine
Live, move, and there are nourished—these are thine;
These from thy wealth thou dost sustain; from thee
Fair babes are born, and fruits on every tree
Hang ripe and large, revered Divinity!

  The life of mortal men beneath thy sway
Is held; thy power both gives and takes away!
Happy are they whom thy mild favours nourish;
All things unstinted round them grow and flourish.
For them endures the life-sustaining field
Its load of harvest, and their cattle yield
Large increase, and their house with wealth is filled.
Such honoured dwell in cities fair and free,
The homes of lovely women, prosperously;
Their sons exult in youth's new budding gladness,
And their fresh daughters free from care or sadness,
With bloom-inwoven dance and happy song,
On the soft flowers the meadow-grass among,
Leap round them sporting—such delights by thee
Are given, rich Power, revered Divinity.

Mother of gods, thou Wife of starry Heaven,
Farewell! be thou propitious, and be given
A happy life for this brief melody,
Nor thou nor other songs shall unremembered be

P. B. SHELLEY, 1818

ANACREON

Ode XXXIII

(*a*)

Downward was the wheeling Bear
Driven by the Waggoner:
Men by powerful sleep opprest,
Gave their busie troubles rest:
Love, in this still depth of night,
Lately at my house did light;
Where perceiving all fast lockt,
At the door he boldly knockt.
'Who's that,' said I, 'that does keep
Such a noise, and breaks my sleep?'
'Ope,' saith Love, 'for pity hear;
'Tis a childe, thou need'st not fear,
Wet and weary, from his way
Led by this dark night astray.'
With compassion this I heard;
Light I struck; the door unbarr'd:
Where a little Boy appears,
Who wings, bow, and quiver bears;
Near the fire I made him stand,
With my own I chaft his hand;
And with kindly busie care
Wrung the chill drops from his hair:
When well warm'd he was, and dry,
'Now,' saith he, ''tis time to try
If my bow no hurt did get,
For methinks the string is wet.'
With that, drawing it, a dart
He let fly that pierc'd my heart:

Leaping then, and laughing said,
'Come my friend, with me be glad;
For my Bow thou see'st is sound
Since thy heart hath got a wound.'

THOMAS STANLEY, 1651

(b)

'Twas noon of night, when round the pole
The sullen Bear is seen to roll;
And mortals, wearied with the day,
Are slumbering all their cares away:
An infant, at that dreary hour,
Came weeping to my silent bower,
And wak'd me with a piteous prayer,
To shield him from the midnight air.
'And who art thou,' I waking cry,
'That bid'st my blissful visions fly?'
'Ah, gentle sire!' the infant said,
'In pity take me to thy shed;
Nor fear deceit: a lonely child
I wander o'er the gloomy wild.
Chill drops the rain, and not a ray
Illumes the drear and misty way!'

 I heard the baby's tale of woe;
I heard the bitter night-winds blow,
And sighing for his piteous fate,
I trimm'd my lamp and op'd the gate.
'Twas Love! the little wandering sprite,
His pinion sparkled through the night.
I knew him by his bow and dart;
I knew him by my fluttering heart.
Fondly I take him in, and raise
The dying embers' cheering blaze;
Press from his dank and clinging hair
The crystals of the freezing air,
And in my hand and bosom hold
His little fingers thrilling cold.

 And now the embers' genial ray
Had warm'd his anxious fears away;

'I pray thee,' said the wanton child,
(My bosom trembled as he smil'd,)
'I pray thee let me try my bow,
For through the rain I've wander'd so,
That much I fear, the midnight shower
Has injured its elastic power.'
The fatal bow the urchin drew;
Swift from the string the arrow flew;
As swiftly flew as glancing flame,
And to my inmost spirit came!
'Fare thee well,' I heard him say,
As laughing wild he wing'd away;
'Fare thee well, for now I know
The rain has not relax'd my bow;
It still can send a thrilling dart,
As thou shalt own with all thy heart!'

THOMAS MOORE, 1800

CATULLUS

Ode XXXI

(*a*)

Gem of all isthmuses and isles that lie,
Fresh or salt water's children, in clear lake
Or ampler ocean, with what joy do I
Approach thee, Sirmio. Oh! Am I awake,
Or dream that once again my eye beholds
Thee, and has looked its last on Thynian wolds?
Sweetest of sweets to me that pastime seems,
When the mind drops her burden: when—the pain
Of travel past—our own cot we regain
And nestle on the pillow of our dreams!
'Tis this one thought that cheers us as we roam.
Hail, O fair Sirmio! Joy, thy lord is here!
Joy too, ye waters of the Garda Mere!
And ring out, all ye laughter-peals of home.

C. S. CALVERLEY, 1862

(b)

Sirmio, thou dearest dear of strands
That Neptune strokes in lake and sea,
With what high joy from stranger lands
Doth thy old friend set foot on thee!
Yea, barely seems it true to me
That no Bithynia holds me now,
But calmly and assuringly
Around me stretchest homely Thou.

Is there a scene more sweet than when
Our clinging cares are undercast,
And, worn by alien moils and men,
The long untrodden sill repassed,
We press the pined for couch at last,
And find a full repayment there?
Then hail, sweet Sirmio; thou that wast,
And art, mine own unrivalled Fair!

THOMAS HARDY, 1887

VIRGIL

Aeneid VI, 269–294

(a)

Obscure they went through dreary shades, that led
Along the waste dominions of the dead.
Thus wander travellers in woods by night,
By the moon's doubtful and malignant light,
When Jove in dusky clouds involves the skies,
And the faint crescent shoots by fits before their eyes.
Just in the gate, and in the jaws of hell,
Revengeful Cares and sullen Sorrows dwell;
And pale Diseases, and repining Age,
Want, Fear, and Famine's unresisted rage;
Here Toils, and Death, and Death's half-brother Sleep
(Forms terrible to view), their sentry keep;
With anxious Pleasures of a guilty mind;
Deep Frauds before, and open Force behind;

The Furies' iron beds; and Strife, that shakes
Her hissing tresses, and unfolds her snakes.
Full in the midst of this infernal road
An elm displays her dusky arms abroad:
The god of sleep there hides his heavy head,
And empty dreams on every leaf are spread.
Of various forms unnumbered spectres more,
Centaurs, and double shapes, besiege the door.
Before the passage, horrid Hydra stands,
And Briareus with all his hundred hands;
Gorgons, Geryon with his triple frame,
And vain Chimæra vomits empty flame.
The chief unsheathed his shining steel, prepared,
Though seized with sudden fear, to force the guard,
Offering his brandished weapon at their face,
Had not the Sibyl stopped his eager pace,
And told him what those empty phantoms were—
Forms without bodies, and impassive air.

JOHN DRYDEN, 1697

(b)

They went obscure in lowering lone night
Through lodges of King Dis, untenanted,—
Featureless lands. Thus goes a forest pathway
Beneath the curst light of the wav'ring moon,
When Jove has gloomed the sky, and pitchy dark
Uncoloured all the world. In Hell's first reach
Fronting the very vestibule of Orcus
Griefs and the Cares have set their couches down,—
The vengeful Cares. There pale Diseases dwell,
Sad Eld and Fear and loathsome Poverty
And Hunger, that bad counsellor,—dire shapes—
And Death and Toil, and Sleep brother of Death
And soul-corrupting joys. Opposed he viewed
War the great murderer, and those steel bowers
The Furies deck for bridal, and Discord
Daft, with blood-ribbons on her serpent hair.
But straight in front a huge black knotted elm
Stood branching: here, they say, the Vain Dreams roost:—

There's not a leaf without one stuck behind!
Next he saw twisted beasts of the old tales:
Centaurs were stabled at the gates: Scyllas
Spread their twin shapes, Briareus his hundred arms.
And Lerna's beast behold hissing out fear,
Chimæra too, who fights with fire, and Gorgons
And Harpies, and a shade with a triple form!
Such was the horror seized Aeneas then
He made to meet their onset with cold steel,
And had th' instructed Sybil not advised
That these were gossamer vitalities
Flitting in stuffless mockery of form,
He'd have leapt on and lashed the empty air.

JAMES ELROY FLECKER, 1910

(c)

They wer' amid the shadows by night in loneliness obscure
Walking forth i' the void and vasty dominion of Ades;
As by an uncertain moonray secretly illumin'd
One goeth in the forest, when heav'n is gloomily clouded,
And black night hath robb'd the colours and beauty from all things.

Here in Hell's very jaws, the threshold of darkening Orcus,
Have the avenging Cares laid their sleepless habitation
Wailing Grief, pallid Infections, and heart-stricken Old-age,
Dismal Fear, unholy Famine, with low-grovelling Want,
Forms of spectral horror, gaunt Toil and Death the devourer,
And death's drowsy brother, Torpor; with whom, an inane rout,
All the Pleasures of Sin; there also the Furies in ambusht
Chamber of iron, afore whose bars wild War bloodyhanded
Raged, and mad Discord high brandished her venomous locks.

Midway of all this tract, with secular arms an immense elm
Reareth a crowd of branches, aneath whose leafy protection
Vain dreams thickly nestle, clinging unto the foliage on high:
And many strange creatures of monstrous form and features
Stable about th' entrance, Centaur and Scylla's abortion,
And hundred-handed Briareus, and Lerna's wild beast
Roaring amain, and clothed in frightful flame the Chimæra,
Gorgons and Harpies, and Pluto's three-bodied ogre.

In terror Aeneas upheld his sword to defend him,
With ready naked point confronting their dreaded onset:
And had not the Sibyl warn'd how these lively spirits were
All incorporeal, flitting in thin maskery of form,
He had assail'd their host, and wounded vainly the void air.

ROBERT BRIDGES, 1916

(d)

Vague forms in lonely darkness, they were going
Through void and shadow, through the empty realm
Like people in a forest, when the moonlight
Shifts with a baleful glimmer, and shadow covers
The sky, and all the colours turn to blackness.
At the first threshold, on the jaws of Orcus,
Grief and avenging Cares have set their couches,
And pale Diseases dwell, and sad Old Age,
Fear, evil-counselling Hunger, wretched Need,
Forms terrible to see, and Death, and Toil,
And Death's own brother, Sleep, and evil Joys,
Fantasies of the mind, and deadly War,
The Furies' iron chambers, Discord, raving,
Her snaky hair entwined in bloody bands.
An elm-tree loomed there, shadowy and huge,
The aged boughs outspread, beneath whose leaves,
Men say, the false dreams cling, thousands and thousands.
And there are monsters in the dooryard, Centaurs,
Scyllas, of double shape, the beast of Lerna,
Hissing most horribly, Briareus,
The hundred-handed giant, a Chimæra
Whose armament is fire, Harpies, and Gorgons,
A triple-bodied giant. In sudden panic
Aeneas drew his sword, the edge held forward,
Ready to rush and flail, however blindly,
Save that his wise companion warned him, saying
They had no substance, they were only phantoms
Flitting about, illusions without body.

ROLFE HUMPHRIES, 1951

VIRGIL

Georgics I, 311–34

(*a*)

Now sing we stormy stars, when autumn weighs
The year, and adds to nights, and shortens days,
And suns declining shine with feeble rays;
What cares must then attend the toiling swain;
Or when the lowering spring, with lavish rain,
Beats down the slender stem and bearded grain,
While yet the head is green, or lightly swelled
With milky moisture, overlooks the field.
E'en when the farmer, now secure of fear,
Sends in the swains to spoil the finished year,
E'en while the reaper fills his greedy hands,
And binds the golden sheaves in brittle bands,
Oft have I seen a sudden storm arise,
From all the warring winds that sweep the skies:
The heavy harvest from the root is torn,
And whirled aloft, the lighter stubble borne:
With such a force the flying rack is driven,
And such a winter wears the face of heaven:
And oft whole sheets descend of sluicy rain,
Sucked by the spongy clouds from off the main:
The lofty skies at once come pouring down,
The promised crop and golden labours drown.
The dikes are filled; and with a roaring sound,
The rising rivers float the nether ground;
And rocks the bellowing voice of boiling seas rebound.
The father of the gods his glory shrouds,
Involved in tempests, and a night of clouds;
And from the middle darkness flashing out,
By fits he deals his fiery bolts about.
Earth feels the motions of her angry god:
Her entrails tremble, and her mountains nod,
And flying beasts in forests seek abode:
Deep horror seizes every human breast;

Their pride is humbled and their fear confessed,
While he from high his rolling thunder throws,
And fires the mountains with repeated blows:
The rocks are from their old foundation rent;
The winds redouble, and the rains augment:
The waves on heaps are dashed against the shore;
And now the woods, and now the billows, roar.

JOHN DRYDEN, 1697

(b)

Am I to tell you next of the storms and stars of Autumn?
The things, when days draw in and summer's heat is abating,
That men must guard against? The dangers of showery spring,
When the prick-eared harvest already bristles along the plains
And when in the green blade the milky grain is swelling?
  Well, often I've seen a farmer lead into his golden fields
The reapers and begin to cut the frail-stalked barley,
And winds arise that moment, starting a free-for-all,
Tearing up by the roots whole swathes of heavy corn
And hurling them high in the air: with gusts black as a hurricane
The storm sent flimsy blades and stubble flying before it.
Often, too, huge columns of water come in the sky
And clouds charged off the deep amass for dirty weather
With rain-squalls black: then the whole sky gives way, falls,
Floods with terrific rain the fertile crops and the labours
Of oxen; filled are the ditches, dry rivers arise in spate
Roaring, the sea foams and seethes up the hissing fjords.
The Father, enthroned in midnight cloud, hurls from a flashing
Right hand his lightning: the whole
Earth trembles at the shock; the beasts are fled, and human
Hearts are felled in panic throughout the nations: on Athos,
Rhodope or the Ceraunian massif his bolt flares down:
The south wind doubles its force and thicker falls the rain:
Now wail the woods with that gale tremendous, now the shores wail.

C. DAY LEWIS, 1940

HORACE

Odes I, v

(a)

What slender youth, bedewed with liquid odours,
Courts thee on roses in some pleasant cave,
   Pyrrha? For whom bind'st thou
    In wreaths thy golden hair,
Plain in thy neatness? Oh, how oft shall he
On faith and changed gods complain, and seas
   Rough with black winds and storms
    Unwonted shall admire!
Who now enjoys thee credulous, all gold;
Who always vacant, always amiable,
   Hopes thee, of flattering gales
    Unmindful. Hapless they
To whom thou untried seem'st fair! Me, in my vowed
Picture, the sacred wall declares t'have hung
   My dank and dropping weeds
    To the stern God of Sea.

                     JOHN MILTON, 1673

(b)

What graceful boy, dripping with rich perfume
Wooes thee 'mong roses in some grotto's shade?
      Pyrrha! for whom
   Dost thou thy yellow tresses braid
In simple neatness artlessly arrayed?
Alas, how oft shall he who credulous dreams
   That all is Truth that truthful seems,
Basks in thy sun, nor doubts that he alone
Shall ever call thy golden grace his own,
Heedless of treacherous gales, and love not tried,—
How oft bewail thy broken faith, and chide
The changeful Gods, and stare with wondering eye
On rough seas blackening 'neath a cloud-swept sky!
   Most miserable they

Whom, falsely fair, thou glitterest to betray!
I, too, have hung on Neptune's hallowed shrine
My picture vowed, and garments dark with brine
To that all-powerful God whom winds and waves obey.

STEPHEN DE VERE, 1885

(c)

Pyrrha, what graceful boy now to thy rosy
couch besprinkled with liquid odours
   down in thy cave art thou tying?
   For whom, sprucely but simply,

curls that gold head?...Ah, how many teardrops
for that too volatile heart of thine he'll be shedding
   and for the changed Fates!
   Unused, he will start back

to see the black winds rousing the sea's anger,
who now delights in thee as pure, kind, golden,
   hopes so to prove thee ever,
   of winds' misfaith unwitting!

But O what grief will blast him unawares!
Already my dank garments, with a votive
   tablet upon the temple wall,
   I've hung up to the ruler of the sea.

G. S. FRASER, 1954

HORACE

Odes I, ix

(a)

Behold yon mountain's hoary height,
   Made higher with new mounts of snow;
Again behold the winter's weight
   Oppress the labouring woods below:
And streams, with icy fetters bound,
Benumb'd and cramp'd to solid ground.

118

With well-heap'd logs dissolve the cold,
   And feed the genial hearth with fires;
Produce the wine, that makes us bold,
   And sprightly wit and love inspires:
For what hereafter shall betide,
God, if 'tis worth his care, provide.

Let him alone, with what he made,
   To toss and turn the world below;
At his command the storms invade;
   The winds by his commission blow;
Till with a nod he bids 'em cease,
And then the calm returns, and all is peace.

To-morrow and her works defy,
   Lay hold upon the present hour,
And snatch the pleasures passing by,
   To put them out of fortune's power:
Nor love, nor love's delights disdain;
Whate'er thou gett'st to-day is gain.

Secure those golden early joys,
   That youth unsour'd with sorrow bears,
Ere withering time the taste destroys,
   With sickness and unwieldy years.
For active sports, for pleasing rest,
This is the time to be possess'd;
The best is but in season best.

The appointed hour of promis'd bliss,
   The pleasing whisper in the dark,
The half unwilling willing kiss,
   The laugh that guides thee to the mark,
When the kind nymph would coyness feign,
And hides but to be found again;
These, these are joys, the gods for youth ordain.

              JOHN DRYDEN, 1693

(*b*)

Seest thou yon mountain laden with deep snow,
The groves beneath their fleecy burthen bow,
The streams, congealed, forget to flow,
Come, thaw the cold, and lay a cheerful pile
  Of fuel on the hearth;
Broach the best cask, and make old winter smile
  With seasonable mirth.

This be our part—let Heaven dispose the rest;
 If Jove command, the winds shall sleep,
 That now wage war upon the foamy deep,
And gentle gales spring from the balmy west.

  E'en let us shift to-morrow as we may,
   When to-morrow's passed away,
   We at least shall have to say,
   We have lived another day;
Your auburn locks will soon be silvered o'er,
Old age is at our heels, and youth returns no more.

       WILLIAM COWPER, 1757

(*c*)

How dazzling white with drifted snow
Soracte stands! The woods below
 Are bowed to breaking with their burden;
The frozen rivers have ceased to flow.

Come, friend, let's drive away the cold:
Pile the logs high as hearth will hold,
 And bring me forth a flask of Sabine,
The strong, the mellow, the four years old.

All else entrust to heaven's will,
Which bids the battling winds be still—
 And waves grow calm, and peace possesses
The ash and cypress upon the hill.

No matter what the morrow prove:
Count each day gain the Powers above
 May grant us. Take what boyhood offers,
The fun and dancing and making love.

Leave gloom for when your hair is grey;
Youth is the time for sport and play—
   Then off to keep your tryst at twilight
And softly prattle an hour away,

Or by a tell-tale laugh to trace
The saucy charmer's hiding-place,
   And snatch a pledge from wrist or finger,
Surrendered with but a feign'd ill grace.

H. RACKHAM, 1950

HORACE

Odes IV, vii

(*a*)

The snow, dissolv'd no more is seen,
The fields and woods, behold! are green;
The changing year renews the plain,
The rivers know their banks again;
The sprightly nymph and naked grace
The mazy dance together trace;
The changing year's successive plan
Proclaims mortality to man;
Rough winter's blasts to spring give way,
Spring yields to summer's sov'reign ray;
Then summer sinks in autumn's reign,
And winter chills the world again;
Her losses soon the moon supplies,
But wretched man when once he lies
Where Priam and his sons are laid,
Is nought but ashes and a shade.
Who knows if Jove, who counts our score,
Will toss us in a morning more?
What with your friend you nobly share,
At least you rescue from your heir.
Not you, Torquatus, boast of Rome,
When Minos once has fix'd your doom,
Or eloquence, or splendid birth,
Or virtue, shall restore to earth.

Hippolytus, unjustly slain,
Diana calls to life in vain;
Nor can the might of Theseus rend
The chains of Hell that hold his friend.

SAMUEL JOHNSON, 1784

(b)

The snows are fled away, leaves on the shaws
  And grasses in the mead renew their birth,
The river to the river-bed withdraws,
  And altered is the fashion of the earth.

The Nymphs and Graces three put off their fear
  And unapparelled in the woodland play,
The swift hour and the brief prime of the year
  Say to the soul, *Thou wast not born for aye.*

Thaw follows frost; hard on the heel of spring
  Treads summer sure to die, for hard on hers
Comes autumn, with his apples scattering;
  Then back to wintertide, when nothing stirs.

But oh, whate'er the sky-led seasons mar,
  Moon upon moon rebuilds it with her beams:
Come *we* where Tullus and where Ancus are,
  And good Aeneas, we are dust and dreams.

Torquatus, if the gods in heaven shall add
  The morrow to the day, what tongue has told?
Feast then thy heart, for what thy heart has had
  The fingers of no heir will ever hold.

When thou descendest once the shades among,
  The stern assize and equal judgement o'er,
Not thy long lineage nor thy golden tongue,
  No, nor thy righteousness, shall friend thee more.

Night holds Hippolytus the pure of stain,
  Diana steads him nothing, he must stay;
And Theseus leaves Pirithöus in the chain
  The love of comrades cannot take away.

A. E. HOUSMAN, 1926

(c)

The snows are gone, grass in the fields is growing
   And foliage on the bough:
Earth's seasons change: the shrinking streams are flowing
   Within their channels low.

Now Nymphs and Graces all unclad may boldly
   Dance in the warmth of spring:
Each year, each hour that hastens night says coldly
   'Life is a passing thing.'

Frost yields to Zephyrs, spring to summer's fever,
   And summer will be sped
When autumn pours her plenteous fruit, and ever
   Comes winter, dull and dead.

Yet with the moons the seasons swiftly waken:
   We, when we once have passed
The way that good and rich and great have taken,
   Are dust and shades at last.

Who knows if God above will add tomorrow
   To this completed day?
What you spend now to keep your soul from sorrow
   No heir can waste away.

When you are dead and Minos once has o'er you
   His grand pronouncement made,
Your eloquence, your birth will not restore you,
   Nor your devotion aid.

Hippolytus was chaste, yet Dian never
   Frees him from night again.
Nor from Pirithöus can Theseus sever
   The links of Lethe's chain.

JAMES MACLEAN TODD, 1955

DANTE

Paradiso, Canto XXXIII, 97–145

(*a*)

With fixed heed, suspense and motionless,
Wondering I gazed; and admiration still
Was kindled as I gazed. It may not be,
That one, who looks upon that light, can turn
To other object, willingly, his view.
For all the good, that will may covet, there
Is summ'd; and all, elsewhere defective found,
Complete. My tongue shall utter now, no more
E'en what remembrance keeps, than could the babe's,
That yet is moisten'd at his mother's breast.
Not that the semblance of the living light
Was changed, (that ever as at first remain'd,)
But that my vision quickening, in that sole
Appearance, still new miracles descried,
And toil'd me with the change. In that abyss
Of radiance, clear and lofty, seem'd, methought,
Three orbs of triple hue, clipt in one bound:
And, from another, one reflected seem'd,
As rainbow is from rainbow: and the third
Seem'd fire, breathed equally from both. O speech!
How feeble and how faint art thou, to give
Conception birth. Yet this to what I saw
Is less than little. O eternal Light!
Sole in Thyself that dwell'st; and of Thyself
Sole understood, past, present, or to come;
Thou smiledst, on that circling, which in Thee
Seem'd as reflected splendour, while I mused;
For I therein, methought, in its own hue
Beheld our image painted: steadfastly
I therefore pored upon the view. As one,
Who versed in geometric lore, would fain
Measure the circle; and, though pondering long
And deeply, that beginning, which he needs,

Finds not: e'en such was I, intent to scan
The novel wonder, and trace out the form,
How to the circle fitted, and therein
How placed: but the flight was not for my wing;
Had not a flash darted athwart my mind,
And, in the spleen, unfolded what it sought.
   Here vigour fail'd the towering fantasy:
But yet the will roll'd onward, like a wheel
In even motion, by the Love impell'd,
That moves the sun in Heaven and all the stars.

H. F. CARY, 1812

(b)

My mind in this wise wholly in suspense,
   Steadfast, immovable, attentive gazed,
   And evermore with gazing grew enkindled.
In presence of that light one such becomes,
   That to withdraw therefrom for other prospect
   It is impossible he e'er consent;
Because the good, which object is of will,
   Is gathered all in this, and out of it
   That is defective which is perfect there.
Shorter henceforward will my language fall
   Of what I yet remember, than an infant's
   Who still his tongue doth moisten at the breast.
Not because more than one unmingled semblance
   Was in the living light on which I looked,
   For it is always what it was before;
But through the sight, that fortified itself
   In me by looking, one appearance only
   To me was ever changing as I changed.
Within the deep and luminous subsistence
   Of the High Light appeared to me three circles,
   Of threefold colour and of one dimension,
And by the second seemed the first reflected
   As Iris is by Iris, and the third
   Seemed fire that equally from both is breathed.
O how all speech is feeble and falls short

125

Of my conceit, and this to what I saw
  Is such, 'tis not enough to call it little!
O Light Eterne, sole in thyself that dwellest,
  Sole knowest thyself, and, known unto thyself
  And knowing, lovest and smilest on thyself!
That circulation, which being thus conceived
  Appeared in thee as a reflected light,
  When somewhat contemplated by mine eyes,
Within itself, of its own very colour
  Seemed to me painted with our effigy,
  Wherefore my sight was all absorbed therein.
As the geometrician, who endeavours
  To square the circle and discovers not,
  By taking thought, the principle he wants,
Even such was I at that new apparition;
  I wished to see how the image to the circle
  Conformed itself, and how it there finds place;
But my own wings were not enough for this,
  Had it not been that then my mind there smote
  A flash of lightning, wherein came its wish.
Here vigour failed the lofty fantasy:
  But now was turning my desire and will,
  Even as a wheel that equally is moved,
The Love which moves the sun and the other stars.

H. W. LONGFELLOW, 1867

(c)

Thus did my mind in the suspense of thought
  Gaze fixedly, all immovable and intent,
  And ever fresh fire from its gazing caught.
Man at that light becometh so content
  That to choose other sight and this reject,
  It is impossible that he consent,
Because the good which is the will's object
  Dwells wholly in it, and that within its pale
  Is perfect, which, without, hath some defect.
Even for my remembrance now must fail
  My words, and less than could an infant's store
  Of speech, who at the pap yet sucks, avail;

Not that within the living light was more
   Than one sole aspect of divine essence,
   Being still for ever as it was before,
But the one semblance, seen with more intense
   A faculty, even as over me there stole
   Change, was itself transfigured to my sense.
Within the clear profound Light's aureole
   Three circles from its substance now appeared,
   Of three colours, and each an equal whole.
One its reflection on the next conferred
   As rainbow upon rainbow, and the two
   Breathed equally the fire that was the third.
To my conception O how frail and few
   My words! and that, to what I looked upon,
   Is such that 'little' is more than is its due.
O Light Eternal, who in thyself alone
   Dwell'st and thyself know'st, and self-understood,
   Self-understanding, smilest on thine own!
That circle which, as I conceived it, glowed
   Within thee like reflection of a flame,
   Being by mine eyes a little longer wooed,
Deep in itself, with colour still the same,
   Seemed with our human effigy to fill,
   Wherefore absorbed in it my sight became.
As the geometer who bends all his will
   To measure the circle, and howsoe'er he try
   Fails, for the principle escapes him still,
Such at this mystery new-disclosed was I,
   Fain to understand how the image doth alight
   Upon the circle, and with its form comply.
But these my wings were fledged not for that flight,
   Save that my mind a sudden glory assailed
   And its wish came revealed to it in that light.
To the high imagination force now failed;
   But like to a wheel whose circling nothing jars
   Already on my desire and will prevailed
The Love that moves the sun and the other stars.
LAURENCE BINYON, 1943

CHAUCER

The Nonne Preestes Tale, 1–16

(a)

There lived, as authors tell, in days of yore,
A widow, somewhat old, and very poor:
Deep in a dell her cottage lonely stood,
Well thatched, and under covert of a wood.
   This dowager, on whom my tale I found,
Since last she laid her husband in the ground,
A simple sober life in patience led,
And had but just enough to buy her bread;
But huswifing the little Heaven had lent,
She duly paid a groat for quarter-rent;
And pinched her belly, with her daughters two,
To bring the year about with much ado.
   The cattle in her homestead were three sows,
An ewe called Mally, and three brinded cows.
Her parlour window stuck with herbs around
Of savoury smell; and rushes strewed the ground.
A maple dresser in her hall she had,
On which full many a slender meal she made,
For no delicious morsel passed her throat;
According to her cloth she cut her coat.
No poignant sauce she knew, no costly treat,
Her hunger gave a relish to her meat.

JOHN DRYDEN, 1699

(b)

Once, long ago, there dwelt a poor old widow
In a small cottage by a little meadow
Beside a grove and standing in a dale.
This widow-woman of whom I tell my tale
Since the sad day when last she was a wife
Had led a very patient, simple life.
Little she had in capital or rent,

But still by making do with what God sent
She kept herself and her two daughters going.
Three hefty sows—no more—were all her showing,
Three cows as well; there was a sheep called Molly.
  Sooty her hall, her kitchen melancholy,
And there she ate full many a slender meal;
There was no sauce piquante to spice her veal,
No dainty morsel ever passed her throat,
According to her cloth she cut her coat.

NEVILL COGHILL, 1951

V

POEMS FOR APPRECIATION

(*see p. iv*)

(1) *Compare the treatment of nature in the two following passages:*

(*a*)

To hear the lark begin his flight,
And, singing, startle the dull night,
From his watch-tower in the skies,
Till the dappled dawn doth rise;
Then to come, in spite of sorrow,
And at my window bid good-morrow,
Through the sweet-brier or the vine,
Or the twisted eglantine;
While the cock, with lively din,
Scatters the rear of darkness thin;
And to the stack, or the barn-door,
Stoutly struts his dames before:
Oft list'ning how the hounds and horn
Cheerly rouse the slumb'ring morn,
From the side of some hoar hill,
Through the high wood echoing shrill:
Sometimes walking, not unseen,
By hedgerow elms, on hillocks green,
Right against the eastern gate
Where the great Sun begins his state,
Robed in flames and amber light,
The clouds in thousand liveries dight;
While the ploughman, near at hand,
Whistles o'er the furrow'd land,
And the milkmaid singeth blithe,
And the mower whets his scythe,
And every shepherd tells his tale
Under the hawthorn in the dale.

(*b*)

I love at early morn, from new-mown swath,
    To see the startled frog his route pursue;
To mark while, leaping o'er the dripping path,
    His bright sides scatter dew,

The early lark that from its bustle flies
　　To hail his matin new;
　　　And watch him to the skies:
To note on hedgerow baulks, in moisture sprent,
　　The jetty snail creep from the mossy thorn,
With earnest heed, and tremulous intent,
　　Frail brother of the morn,
That from the tiny bents and misted leaves
　　Withdraws his timid horn,
　　　And fearful vision weaves:
Or swallow heed on smoke-tanned chimney top,
　　Wont to be first unsealing morning's eye,
Ere yet the bee hath gleaned one wayward drop
　　Of honey on his thigh;
To see him seek morn's airy couch to sing
　　Until the golden sky
　　　Bepaint his russet wing:
And sawning boy by tanning corn espy,
　　With clapping noise to startle birds away,
And hear him bawl to every passer-by
　　To know the hour of day;
And see the uncradled breeze, refreshed and strong,
　　With waking blossoms play,
　　　And breathe aeolian song.

(2) *Compare the following passages as examples of dramatic speech:*

(*a*)

Illustrious England, ancient seat of kings,
Whose chivalry hath royalized thy fame,
That sounding bravely through terrestrial vales
Proclaiming conquests, spoils and victories,
Rings glorious echoes through the farthest world;
What warlike nation, trained in feats of arms,
What barbarous people, stubborn or untamed,
What climate under the meridian signs,
Or frozen zone under his brumal plage,
Erst have not quaked and trembled at the name
Of Britain and her mighty conquerors?

Her neighbour-nations, as Scotland, Denmark, France,
Awed with their deeds and jealous of her arms,
Have begged defensive and offensive leagues.
Thus Europe, rich and mighty in her kings,
Hath feared brave England, dreadful in her kings
And now, to eternize Albion's champions,
Equivalent with Trojans' ancient fame,
Comes lovely Edward from Jerusalem,
Veering before the wind, ploughing the sea,
His strechèd sails filled with the breath of men,
That through the world admire his manliness.

(b)

This royal throne of kings, this scepter'd isle,
This earth of majesty, this seat of Mars,
This other Eden, demi-paradise,
This fortress built by Nature for herself
Against infection and the hand of war,
This happy breed of men, this little world,
This precious stone set in the silver sea,
Which serves it in the office of a wall,
Or as a moat defensive to a house,
Against the envy of less happier lands,
This blessed plot, this earth, this realm, this England,
This nurse, this teeming womb of royal kings,
Feared by their breed and famous by their birth,
Renownèd for their deeds as far from home—
For Christian service and true chivalry—
As is the sepulchre in stubborn Jewry
Of the world's ransom blessèd Mary's Son:
This land of such dear souls, this dear, dear land,
Dear for her reputation through the world,
Is now leased out—I die pronouncing it—
Like to a tenement, or pelting farm:
England, bound in with the triumphant sea,
Whose rocky shore beats back the envious siege,
Of watery Neptune, is now bound in with shame,
With inky blots, and rotten parchment bonds:

That England, that was wont to conquer others
Hath made a shameful conquest of itself.
Ah! would the scandal vanish with my life,
How happy then were my ensuing death.

(3) *If you were compiling an anthology of poetry would you include any of these poems? Give reasons for your choice or rejection of each poem.*

(*a*)

What bird so sings, yet so does wail?
O 'tis the ravished nightingale.
'Jug, jug, jug, jug, tereu', she cries,
And still her woes at midnight rise.
Brave prick-song! who is't now we hear?
None but the lark so shrill and clear;
Now at heaven's gates she claps her wings,
The morn not waking till she sings.
Hark, hark, with what a pretty throat,
Poor robin redbreast tunes his note;
Hark how the jolly cuckoos sing,
Cuckoo to welcome in the spring!
Cuckoo to welcome in the spring!

(*b*)

When first we hear the shy-come nightingales,
They seem to mutter o'er their songs in fear,
And, climb we e'er so soft the spinney rails,
All stops as if no bird was anywhere.
The kindled bushes with the young leaves thin
Let curious eyes to search a long way in,
Until impatience cannot see or hear
The hidden music; gets but little way
Upon the path—when up the songs begin,
Full loud a moment and then low again.
But when a day or two confirms her stay
Boldly she sings and loud for half the day;
And soon the village brings the woodman's tale
Of having heard the new-come nightingale.

(c)

What voice of gladness, hark!
    In heaven is ringing?
From the sad fields the lark
    Is upward winging.

High through the mournful mist that blots our day
Their songs betray them soaring in the grey.
                See them! Nay, they
In sunlight swim; above the furthest stain
Of cloud attain; their hearts in music rain
                Upon the plain.

    Sweet birds, far out of sight
        Your songs of pleasure
    Dome us with joy as bright
        As heaven's best azure.

(d)

Robin on a leafless bough,
    Lord in Heaven, how he sings!
Now cold Winter's cruel wind
    Makes playmates of poor, dead things.

How he sings for joy this morn!
    How his breast doth pant and glow!
Look you how he stands and sings,
    Half-way up his legs in snow!

If these crumbs of bread were pearls,
    And I had no bread at home,
He should have them for that song;
    Pretty Robin Redbreast, Come.

(e)

O blithe New-comer! I have heard,
    I hear thee and rejoice:
O Cuckoo! shall I call thee Bird,
    Or but a wandering Voice?

While I am lying on the grass
    Thy twofold shout I hear;
From hill to hill it seems to pass,
    At once far off and near.

Though babbling only to the vale
    Of sunshine and of flowers,
Thou bringest unto me a tale
    Of visionary hours.

Thrice welcome, darling of the Spring!
    Even yet thou art to me
No bird, but an invisible thing,
    A voice, a mystery;

The same whom in my school-boy days
    I listen'd to; that Cry
Which made me look a thousand ways
    In bush, and tree, and sky,

To seek thee did I often rove
    Through woods and on the green;
And thou wert still a hope, a love;
    Still long'd for, never seen!

And I can listen to thee yet;
    Can lie upon the plain
And listen, till I do beget
    That golden time again.

O blessèd Bird! the earth we pace
    Again appears to be
An unsubstantial, faery place,
    That is fit home for Thee!

(4) *Here are two versions of the same poem. What reasons can you find
for the changes in the second poem?*

(a)

A hiding tuft, a greenbarked yewtree,
    Holds the roof,
Dearest spot! The oaktree guards me,
    Tempestproof.

Full of bounty, there's an apple
   Like an inn!
A fistful of a bush of hazel,
   Branching, green.

A peaceful troop, a country gathering
   Pays a call,
And the foxes come to join them,
   Best of all.

To what feasts the woods invite me
   All about!
Water pure and herbs and cresses,
   Salmon, trout.

All a man could ask of comfort
   Round me grows
Haws and yewberries and strawberries,
   Nuts and sloes.

And when summer spreads its mantle,
   There's a sight!
Marjoram and leeks and pignuts
   Green and bright.

Bees and beetles, nature's singers,
   Croon and strum,
Geese pass over, duck in autumn,
   Dark streams hum.

In the year's most brilliant weather
   Heifers low
Through green fields, not harsh nor laboured,
   Tranquil, slow.

(*b*)

A hiding tuft, a greenbarked yewtree,
   Spreads its roof,
An oak keeps this dear spot and me
   Tempestproof.

I can fetch an apple from a tree
   Like an inn
Or can fill my fists where hazels
   Block the scene.

Inquirers from a neighbouring country
   Pay a call,
And the foxes come to join them,
   Best of all.

To what a diet the woods invite me
   All about!
Water pure and herbs and cresses,
   Salmon and trout.

All a man could ask of comfort
   Round me grows
Hips and haws and strawberries,
   Nuts and sloes.

And when summer spreads its mantle,
   There's a sight!
Marjoram and leeks and pignuts
   Show green and bright.

Bees and beetles, natural singers,
   Croon and strum,
Geese pass over, duck in autumn,
   Dark streams hum.

In the year's most brilliant weather
   Heifers low
Through green fields, not driven and beaten,
   Tranquil, slow.

(5) *Compare the following passages, indicating differences of tone and manner:*

(a)

In the worst inn's worst room, with mat half-hung,
The floors of plaister, and the walls of dung,
On once a flock-bed, but repair'd with straw,
With tape-ty'd curtains, never meant to draw,

The George and Garter dangling from that bed
Where tawdry yellow strove with dirty red,
Great *Villiers* lies—alas! how chang'd from him,
That life of pleasure, and that soul of whim!...
No Wit to flatter left of all his store!
No Fool to laugh at, which he valu'd more.
There, Victor of his health, of fortune, friends,
And fame, this lord of useless thousands ends.

(b)

Such is that room which one rude beam divides,
And naked rafters form the sloping sides;
Where the vile bands that bind the thatch are seen,
And lath and mud are all that lie between;
Save one dull pane, that, coarsely patch'd, gives way
To the rude tempest, yet excludes the day:
Here, on a matted flock, with dust o'erspread,
The drooping wretch reclines his languid head;
For him no hand the cordial cup applies,
Or wipes the tear that stagnates in his eyes;
No friends with soft discourse his pain beguile,
Or promise hope till sickness wears a smile.

(6) *Examine the use of metaphor and personification in these poems and say whether the poet's meaning is helped or obscured.*

(a)

Yes, thou art gone! and round me too the night
    In ever-nearing circle weaves her shade.
        I see her veil draw soft across the day,
    I feel her slowly chilling breath invade
        The cheek grown thin, the brown hair sprent with grey;
            I feel her finger light
Laid pausefully upon life's headlong train;
        The foot less prompt to meet the morning dew,
        The heart less bounding at emotion new,
    And hope, once crush'd, less quick to spring again.

And long the way appears, which seem'd so short
　　To the unpractis'd eye of sanguine youth;
　　　And high the mountain-tops, in cloudy air,
　　The mountain-tops where is the throne of Truth,
　　　Tops in life's morning-sun so bright and bare!
　　　　　Unbreachable the fort
　　Of the long-batter'd world uplifts its wall.
　　　And strange and vain the earthly turmoil grows,
　　　And near and real the charm of thy repose,
And night as welcome as a friend would fall.

(b)

　　In vain to me the smiling mornings shine,
　　　And reddening Phoebus lifts his golden fire;
　　The birds in vain their amorous descant join,
　　　Or cheerful fields resume their green attire.
　　These ears, alas! for other notes repine,
　　　A different object do these eyes require:
　　My lonely anguish melts no heart but mine;
　　　And in my breast the imperfect joys expire.
　　Yet morning smiles the busy race to cheer,
　　　And new-born pleasures bring to happier men:
　　The fields to all their wonted tribute bear:
　　　To warm their little loves the birds complain.
　　I fruitless mourn to him that cannot hear,
　　　And weep the more, because I weep in vain.

(7) *Compare and contrast the following poems in point of style, feeling and intention:*

(a)

　　I heard a thousand blended notes,
　　While in a grove I sate reclined,
　　In that sweet mood when pleasant thoughts
　　Bring sad thoughts to the mind.

　　To her fair works did Nature link
　　The human soul that through me ran;
　　And much it grieved my heart to think
　　What man has made of man.

Through primrose tufts, in that green bower,
The periwinkle trailed its wreaths;
And 'tis my faith that every flower
Enjoys the air it breathes.

The birds around me hopped and played,
Their thoughts I cannot measure:—
But the least motion which they made,
It seemed a thrill of pleasure.

The budding twigs spread out their fan,
To catch the breezy air;
And I must think, do all I can,
That there was pleasure there.

If this belief from heaven be sent,
If such be Nature's holy plan,
Have I not reason to lament
What man has made of man?

(b)

Heart-halt and spirit-lame,
    City-opprest,
Unto this wood I came
    As to a nest;
Dreaming that sylvan peace
Offered the harrowed ease—
Nature a soft release
    From men's unrest.

But, having entered in,
    Great growth and small
Show them to men akin—
    Combatants all!
Sycamore shoulders oak,
Bines the slim saplings yoke,
Ivy-spun halters choke
    Elms stout and tall.

Touches from ash, O wych,
    Sting you like scorn!

You, too, brave hollies, twitch
    Sidelong from thorn.
Even the rank poplars bear
Illy a rival's air,
Cankering in black despair
    If overborne.

Since, then, no grace I find
    Taught me of trees,
Turn I back to my kind,
    Worthy as these.
There at least smiles abound,
There discourse trills around
There, now and then, are found
    Life-loyalties.

(8) *Compare the following passages, and try to explain in what respects one is better than the other:*

(*a*)

Nor was his name unheard or unador'd
In ancient Greece, and in Ausonian land
Men call'd him Mulciber; and how he fell
From Heav'n they fabl'd, thrown by angry Jove
Sheer o'er the Chrystal Battlements; from Morn
To Noon he fell, from Noon to dewy Eve,
A Summer's day; and with the setting Sun
Dropt from the Zenith like a falling Star
On Lemnos th' Ægæan Ile: thus they relate,
Erring; for he with his rebellious rout
Fell long before.

(*b*)

Falling, falling! Los fell and fell,
Sunk precipitant, heavy, down, down,
Times on times, night on night, day on day;
Truth has bounds, Error none: falling, falling;
Years on years, and ages on ages
Still he fell thro' the void, still a void
Found for falling day and night without end;

For though day or night was not, their spaces
Were measur'd by his incessant whirls
In the horrid vacuity bottomless.

9) *Appraise the following two poems:*

(*a*)

There was an Indian, who had known no change,
 Who strayed content along a sunlit beach
Gathering shells. He heard a sudden strange
 Commingled noise: looked up; and gasped for speech.
For in the bay, where nothing was before,
 Moving on the sea, by magic, huge canoes,
With bellying cloths on poles, and not one oar,
 And fluttering coloured signs and clambering crews.

And he, in fear, this naked man alone,
 His fallen hands forgetting all their shells,
His lips gone pale, knelt low behind a stone,
 And stared, and saw, and did not understand,
Columbus's doom-burdened caravels
 . Slant to the shore, and all their seamen land.

(*b*)

Much have I travelled in the realms of gold,
 And many goodly states and kingdoms seen;
 Round many western islands have I been
Which bards in fealty to Apollo hold.
Oft of one wide expanse had I been told,
 That deep-browed Homer ruled as his demesne:
 Yet did I never breathe its pure serene
Till I heard Chapman speak out loud and bold:
Then felt I like some watcher of the skies
 When a new planet swims into his ken;
Or like stout Cortez, when with eagle eyes
 He stared at the Pacific—and all his men
Looked at each other with a wild surmise—
 Silent, upon a peak in Darien.

(10) *Compare and contrast the two following poems:*

(a)

Since there's no help, come let us kiss and part;
Nay, I have done, you get no more of me;
And I am glad, yea, glad with all my heart,
That thus so cleanly I myself can free;
Shake hands for ever, cancel all our vows,
And when we meet at any time again,
Be it not seen in either of our brows
That we one jot of former love retain.
Now at the last gasp of love's latest breath,
When his pulse failing, passion speechless lies,
When faith is kneeling by his bed of death,
And innocence is closing up his eyes,
Now if thou would'st, when all have given him over,
From death to life thou might'st him yet recover.

(b)

All's over, then; does truth sound bitter
⠀⠀⠀⠀As one at first believes?
Hark, 'tis the sparrows' good-night twitter
⠀⠀⠀⠀About your cottage eaves!

And the leaf-buds on the vine are woolly,
⠀⠀⠀⠀I noticed that, to-day;
One day more bursts them open fully
⠀⠀⠀⠀—You know the red turns grey.

To-morrow we meet the same then, dearest?
⠀⠀⠀⠀May I take your hand in mine?
Mere friends are we,—well, friends the merest
⠀⠀⠀⠀Keep much that I'll resign:

For each glance of that eye so bright and black,
⠀⠀⠀⠀Though I keep with heart's endeavour,—
Your voice, when you wish the snowdrops back,
⠀⠀⠀⠀Though it stay in my soul for ever!—

Yet I will but say what mere friends say,
    Or only a thought stronger;
I will hold your hand but as long as all may,
    Or so very little longer!

(11) *Which of these two poems do you prefer, and why?*

(*a*)

Behold her, single in the field,
Yon solitary Highland lass!
Reaping and singing by herself;
Stop here, or gently pass!
Alone she cuts and binds the grain,
And sings a melancholy strain;
Oh, listen! for the vale profound
Is overflowing with the sound.

No nightingale did ever chaunt
More welcome notes to weary bands
Of travellers in some shady haunt,
Among Arabian sands:
A voice so thrilling ne'er was heard
In spring-time from the cuckoo-bird,
Breaking the silence of the seas
Among the farthest Hebrides.

Will no one tell me what she sings?
Perhaps the plaintive numbers flow
For old, unhappy, far-off things,
And battles long ago:
Or is it some more humble lay,
Familiar matter of to-day?
Some natural sorrow, loss, or pain,
That has been, and may be again?

Whate'er the theme, the maiden sang
As if her song could have no ending;
I saw her singing at her work,
And o'er the sickle bending;
I listen'd, till I had my fill;

And, as I mounted up the hill,
The music in my heart I bore,
Long after it was heard no more.

(*b*)

There was never a sound beside the wood but one,
And that was my long scythe whispering to the ground.
What was it it whispered? I knew not well myself;
Perhaps it was something about the heat of the sun,
Something, perhaps, about the lack of sound—
And that was why it whispered and did not speak.
It was no dream of the gift of idle hours,
Or easy gold at the hand of fay or elf:
Anything more than the truth would have seemed too weak
To the earnest love that laid the swale in rows,
Not without feeble-pointed spikes of flowers
(Pale orchises), and scared a bright green snake.
The fact is the sweetest dream that labour knows.
My long scythe whispered and left the hay to make.

(12) *Compare these two poems:*

(*a*)

The warm sun is failing, the bleak wind is wailing,
The bare boughs are sighing, the pale flowers are dying;
And the Year
On the earth her death-bed, in a shroud of leaves dead,
Is lying.
Come, Months, come away,
From November to May,
In your saddest array;
Follow the bier
Of the dead cold Year,
And like dim shadows watch by her sepulchre.

The chill rain is falling, the nipped worm is crawling,
The rivers are swelling, the thunder is knelling
For the Year;
The blithe swallows are flown, and the lizards each gone
To his dwelling.

Come, Months, come away;
Put on white, black and grey;
Let your light sisters play—
Ye, follow the bier
Of the dead cold Year,
And make her grave green with tear on tear.

(b)

I saw old Autumn in the misty morn
Stand shadowless like Silence, listening
To silence, for no lonely bird would sing
Into his hollow ear from woods forlorn,
Nor lowly hedge nor solitary thorn;
Shaking his languid locks all dewy bright
With tangled gossamer that fell by night,
  Pearling his coronet of golden corn.

Where are the songs of Summer? With the sun,
Oping the dusky eyelids of the south,
Till shade and silence waken up as one,
And Morning sings with a warm odorous mouth.
Where are the merry birds? Away, away,
On panting wings through the inclement skies,
  Lest owls should prey
  Undazzled at noonday,
And tear with horny beak their lustrous eyes.

Where are the blossoms of Summer? In the west,
Blushing their last to the last sunny hours
When the mild Eve by sudden Night is prest
Like a tearful Proserpine, snatched from her flowers
  To a most gloomy breast.
Where is the pride of Summer—the green prime—
The many, many leaves all twinkling? Three
  On the mossed elm; three on the naked lime
Trembling—and one upon the old oak tree.
Where is the Dryad's immortality?
Gone into mournful cypress and dark yew,
Or wearing the long gloomy Winter through
  In the smooth holly's green eternity.

(13) *Write a careful comparison of these two poems:*

(*a*)

Ethereal minstrel! pilgrim of the sky!
Dost thou despise the earth where cares abound?
Or, while the wings aspire, are heart and eye
Both with thy nest upon the dewy ground?
Thy nest which thou canst drop into at will,
Those quivering wings composed, that music still!

Leave to the nightingale her shady wood;
A privacy of glorious light is thine;
Whence thou dost pour upon the world a flood
Of harmony, with instinct more divine;
Type of the wise who soar, but never roam;
True to the kindred points of Heaven and Home!

To the last point of vision, and beyond,
Mount, daring warbler!—that love-prompted strain,
('Twixt thee and thine a never-failing bond).
Thrills not the less the bosom of the plain:
Yet might'st thou seem, proud privilege! to sing
All independent of the leafy spring.

(*b*)

Above the russet clods the corn is seen
Sprouting its spiry points of tender green,
Where squats the hare, to terrors wide awake,
Like some brown clod the harrows failed to break.
Opening their golden caskets to the sun,
The buttercups make schoolboys eager run,
To see who shall be first to pluck the prize—
Up from their hurry see the Skylark flies,
And o'er her half-formed nest, with happy wings,
Winnows the air till in the cloud she sings,
Then hangs a dust spot in the sunny skies,
And drops and drops till in her nest she lies,
Which they unheeded passed—not dreaming then
That birds, which flew so high, would drop again
To nest upon the ground, which anything
May come at to destroy. Had they the wing

Like such a bird, themselves would be too proud
And build on nothing but a passing cloud!
As free from danger as the heavens are free
From pain and toil, there would they build and be,
And sail about the world to scenes unheard
Of and unseen,—O were they but a bird!
So think they while they listen to its song,
And smile and fancy and so pass along;
While its low nest, moist with the dews of morn,
Lies safely, with the leveret, in the corn.

(14) *Examine these two versions of the same poem, say which you consider the revised version, and give your reasons.*

(*a*)

Two pewits sport and cry
Under the after sunset sky,
Whiter than the moon on high
That rides the black surge in the sky,
Than the pool it is mirrored by,
The only light under the sky;
Blacker than the earth. Their cry
Makes the sole sound under the sky.
They alone move, low or high.
And merrily they cry,
To the mischievous dark sky,
Plunging earthward, tossing high
They care not for the sigh
Of the traveller wondering why
So merrily they cry and fly,
They choose not between earth and sky,
While the moon's quarter silently
Rides, and earth rests as silently.

(*b*)

Under the after-sunset sky
Two pewits sport and cry,
More white than is the moon on high
Riding the dark surge silently;

More black than earth. Their cry
Is the one sound under the sky,
They alone move, now low, now high,
And merrily they cry
To the mischievous Spring sky,
Plunging earthward, tossing high,
Over the ghost who wonders why
So merrily they cry and fly,
Nor choose 'twixt earth and sky,
While the moon's quarter silently
Rides, and earth rests as silently.

(15) *Compare the manner of expression of these two passages:*

(*a*)

The Cock is crowing,
The stream is flowing,
The small birds twitter,
The lake doth glitter,
The green field sleeps in the sun;
The oldest and youngest
Are at work with the strongest;
The cattle are grazing,
Their heads never raising;
There are forty feeding like one!

Like an army defeated
The snow hath retreated,
And now doth fare ill
On the top of the bare hill;
The Ploughboy is whooping—anon—anon:
There's joy in the mountains;
There's life in the fountains;
Small clouds are sailing,
Blue sky prevailing;
The rain is over and gone!

(b)

A touch, a kiss! the charm was snapt.
   There rose a noise of striking clocks,
And feet that ran, and doors that clapt,
   And barking dogs, and crowing cocks;
A fuller light illumined all,
   A breeze through all the garden swept,
A sudden hubbub shook the hall,
   And sixty feet the fountain leapt.

The hedge broke in, the banner blew,
   The butler drank, the steward scrawl'd,
The fire shot up, the martin flew,
   The parrot scream'd, the peacock squall'd,
The maid and page renew'd their strife,
   The palace bang'd and buzz'd and clackt,
And all the long-pent stream of life
   Dash'd downward in a cataract.

(16) *Analyse the different effects produced on you by each of the following poems:*
(a)

We are slumberous poppies,
   Lords of Lethe downs,
Some awake, and some asleep,
   Sleeping in our crowns.
What perchance our dreams may know,
Let our serious beauty show.

Central depth of purple,
   Leaves more bright than rose,
Who shall tell what brightest thought
   Out of darkest grows?
Who, through what funereal pain,
Souls to love and peace again?

Visions aye are on us,
   Unto eyes of power,

Pluto's always setting sun,
   And Proserpine's bower:
There, like bees, the pale souls come
For our drink with drowsy hum.

Taste, ye mortals, also;
   Milky-hearted, we;
Taste, but with a reverent care;
   Active-patient be.
Too much gladness brings to gloom
Those who on the gods presume.

(b)

The sleep-flower sways in the wheat its head,
Heavy with dreams, as that with bread:
The goodly grain and the sun-flushed sleeper
The reaper reaps, and Time the reaper.

I hang mid men my needless head,
And my fruit is dreams, as theirs is bread:
The goodly men and the sun-hazed sleeper
Time shall reap, but after the reaper
The world shall glean of me, me the sleeper.

(17) *Compare the following passages as examples of dramatic speech:*

(a)

O you hard hearts, you cruel men of Rome,
Knew you not Pompey? Many a time and oft
Have you climb'd up to walls and battlements,
To towers and windows, yea, to chimney-tops,
Your infants in your arms, and there have sat
The livelong day, with patient expectation,
To see great Pompey pass the streets of Rome:
And when you saw his chariot but appear,
Have you not made an universal shout,
That Tiber trembled underneath her banks,
To hear the replication of your sounds
Made in her concave shores?

154

And do you now put on your best attire?
And do you now cull out a holiday?
And do you now strew flowers in his way,
That comes in triumph over Pompey's blood?

(b)

All tongues speak of him, and the bleared sights
Are spectacled to see him: your prattling nurse
Into a rapture lets her baby cry,
While she chats him; the kitchen malkin pins
Her richest lockram 'bout her reechy neck,
Clambering the walls to eye him: stalls, bulks, windows,
Are smother'd up, leads fill'd, and ridges hors'd
With variable complexions, all agreeing
In earnestness to see him: seld-shown flamens
Do press among the popular throngs, and puff
To win a vulgar station: our veil'd dames
Commit the war of white and damask, in
Their nicely-gawded cheeks, to the wanton spoil
Of Phoebus' burning kisses: such a pother
As if that whatsoever god who leads him
Were slily crept into his human powers,
And gave him graceful posture.

(18) *Examine the following poems, and say what you find of interest
in each:*
(a)

Spring, the sweet Spring, is the year's pleasant king;
Then blooms each thing, then maids dance in a ring,
Cold doth not sting, the pretty birds do sing—
    Cuckoo, jug-jug, pu-we, to-witta-woo!

The palm and may make country houses gay,
Lambs frisk and play, the shepherds pipe all day,
And we hear aye birds tune this merry lay—
    Cuckoo, jug-jug, pu-we, to-witta-woo!

The fields breathe sweet, the daisies kiss our feet,
Young lovers meet, old wives a-sunning sit,

In every street these tunes our ears do greet—
    Cuckoo, jug-jug, pu-we, to-witta-woo!
      Spring the sweet Spring!

(*b*)

Now fades the last long streak of snow,
    Now burgeons every maze of quick
    About the flowering squares, and thick
By ashen roots the violets blow.

Now rings the woodland loud and long,
    The distance takes a lovelier hue,
    And drown'd in yonder living blue
The lark becomes a sightless song.

Now dance the lights on lawn and lea,
    The flocks are whiter down the vale,
    And milkier every milky sail
On winding stream or distant sea;

Where now the seamew pipes, or dives
    In yonder greening gleam, and fly
    The happy birds, that change their sky
To build and brood; that live their lives

From land to land; and in my breast
    Spring wakens too; and my regret
    Becomes an April violet,
And buds and blossoms like the rest.

(*c*)

O thou with dewy locks, who lookest down
Through the clear windows of the morning, turn
Thine angel eyes upon our western isle,
Which in full choir hails thy approach, O Spring!

The hills tell one another, and the listening
Valleys hear; all our longing eyes are turn'd
Up to thy bright pavilions: issue forth
And let thy holy feet visit our clime!

156

Come o'er the eastern hills, and let our winds
Kiss thy perfumèd garments; let us taste
Thy morn and evening breath; scatter thy pearls
Upon our lovesick land that mourns for thee.

O deck her forth with thy fair fingers; pour
Thy soft kisses on her bosom; and put
Thy golden crown upon her languish'd head,
Whose modest tresses were bound up for thee.

(d)

Now the full-throated daffodils,
Our trumpeters in gold,
Call resurrection from the ground
And bid the year be told.

To-day the almond-tree turns pink,
The first flush of spring;
Winds loll and gossip through the town
Her secret whispering.

Now too the bird must try his voice
Upon the morning air;
Down drowsy avenues he cries
A novel great affair.

He tells of royalty to be;
How with her train of rose,
Summer to coronation comes
Through waving wild hedgerows.

To-day crowds quicken in a street,
The fish leaps in the flood:
Look there, gasometer rises,
And here boughs swell to bud.

For our love's luck, our stowaway,
Stretches in his cabin;
Our youngster joy, barely conceived
Shows up beneath the skin.

Our joy was but a gusty thing
Without sinew or wit,
An infant flyaway; but now
We make a man of it.

(19) *Compare the following poems, paying particular attention t*
diction and imagery:
(a)

Flowers of the willow-herb are wool;
Flowers of the briar berries red;
Speeding their seed as the breeze may rule,
Flowers of the thistle loosen the thread.
Flowers of the clematis drip in beard,
Slack from the fir-tree youngly climbed;
Chaplets in air, flies foliage seared;
Heeled upon earth, lie clusters rimed.

Where were skies of the mantle stained
Orange and scarlet, a coat of frieze
Travels from North till day has waned,
Tattered, soaked in the ditch's dyes;
Tumbles the rook under gray or slate;
Else unfolds us, damps to the bone;
Narrows the world to my neighbour's gate;
Paints me Life as a wheezy crone.

Now seems none but the spider lord;
Star in circle his web waits prey,
Silvering bush-mounds, blue brushing sward;
Slow runs the hour, swift flits the ray.
Now to his thread-shroud is he nigh,
Nigh to the tangle where wings are sealed,
He who frolicked the jewelled fly;
All is adroop on the down and the weald.

(b)

This darksome burn, horseback brown,
His rollcock highroad roaring down,
In coop and in comb the fleece of his foam
Flutes, and low to the lake falls home.

A windpuff-bonnet of fawn-froth
Turns and twindles over the broth
Of a pool so pitchblack, fell-frowning,
It rounds and rounds Despair to drowning.

Degged with dew, dappled with dew
Are the groins of the braes that the brook treads through,
Wiry heathpacks, flitches of fern,
And the beadbonny ash that sits over the burn.

What would the world be, once bereft
Of wet and of wildness? Let them be left,
O let them be left, wildness and wet;
Long live the weeds and the wilderness yet.

(20) *Comment on the versification of the following passages:*

(*a*)

In parchments then, large as his fields, hee drawes
Assurances, bigge, as gloss'd civill lawes,
So huge, that men (in our times forwardnesse)
Are Fathers of the Church for writing lesse.
These hee writes not; nor for these written payes,
Therefore spares no length; as in those first dayes
When Luther was profest, He did desire
Short *Pater nosters*, saying as a Fryer
Each day his beads, but having left those lawes,
Addes to Christs prayer, the Power and glory clause.
But when he sells or changes land, he 'impaires
His writings, and (unwatch'd) leaves out, *ses heires*,
As slily as any Commenter goes by
Hard words, or sense; or in Divinity
As controverters, in vouch'd Texts, leave out
Shrewd words, which might against them cleare the doubt.

(*b*)

Then strongly fencing ill-got wealth by law,
Indentures, Cov'nants, Articles they draw,
Large as the fields themselves, and larger far
Than Civil Codes, with all their Glosses are;

So vast, our new Divines, we must confess,
Are Fathers of the Church for writing less.
But let them write for you, each rogue impairs
The deeds, and dext'rously omits, *ses heires*:
No Commentator can more slily pass
O'er a learn'd, unintelligible place;
Or, in quotation, shrewd Divines leave out
Those words, that would against them clear the doubt.
　So Luther thought the Pater-noster long,
When doom'd to say his beads and Even-song;
But having cast his cowl, and left those laws,
Adds to Christ's pray'r, the *Pow'r and Glory* clause.

(21) *Compare the following, stating the attitude of each poet to his subject; say which poem you prefer and give your reasons.*

(*a*)

When maidens such as Hester die,
Their place ye may not well supply,
Though ye among a thousand try,
　　With vain endeavour.

A month or more hath she been dead,
Yet cannot I by force be led
To think upon the wormy bed,
　　And her together.

A springy motion in her gait,
A rising step, did indicate
Of pride and joy no common rate,
　　That flush'd her spirit.

I know not by what name beside
I shall it call:—if 'twas not pride,
It was a joy to that allied,
　　She did inherit.

Her parents held the Quaker rule,
Which doth the human feeling cool,
But she was train'd in Nature's school,
　　Nature had blest her.

A waking eye, a prying mind,
A heart that stirs, is hard to bind,
A hawk's keen sight ye cannot blind,
    Ye could not Hester.

My sprightly neighbour, gone before
To that unknown and silent shore,
Shall we not meet, as heretofore,
    Some summer morning,

When from thy cheerful eyes a ray
Hath struck a bliss upon the day,
A bliss that would not go away,
    A sweet fore-warning?

(b)

Enough: and leave the rest to Fame.
'Tis to commend her but to name.
Courtship, which living she declin'd,
When dead to offer were unkind.
Where never any could speak ill,
Who would officious praises spill?
Nor can the truest wit or friend,
Without detracting, her commend.
To say she liv'd a virgin chaste,
In this age loose and all unlac't;
Nor was, when vice is so allow'd,
Of virtue or asham'd, or proud;
That her soul was on Heaven so bent
No minute but it came and went;
That ready her last debt to pay
She summ'd her life up ev'ry day;
Modest as morn; as mid-day bright;
Gentle as ev'ning; cool as night;
'Tis true: but all so weakly said;
'Twere more significant, *She's Dead*.

(22) *Examine these three successive drafts of Milton's 'Lycidas' and try to account for the changes.*

(*a*)

Bring the rathe primrose that unwedded dies
colouring the pale cheek of unenjoyed love
and the sad flower that strove
to write his own woes in the vermeil grain
next add Narcissus that still weeps in vain
the woodbine and the pansy freaked with jet
the glowing violet
the cowslip wan that hangs his pensive head
and every bud that sorrow's livery wears
let Daffadillies fill their cups with tears
bid Amaranthus all his beauty shed.

(*b*)

Bring the rathe primrose that forsaken dies
the tufted crow-toe and pale Gessamin
the white pink and the pansy freaked with jet
the glowing violet
the musk rose and the garish columbine
with cowslips wan that hang the pensive head
and every flower that sad escutcheon bears
let Daffadillies fill their cups with tears
bid Amaranthus all his beauties shed.

(*c*)

Bring the rathe primrose that forsaken dies,
The tufted crow-toe, and pale jessamine,
The white pink and the pansy freaked with jet,
The glowing violet,
The musk-rose, and the well-attired woodbine,
With cowslips wan that hang the pensive head,
And every flower that sad embroidery wears:
Bid amaranthus all his beauty shed,
And daffadillies fill their cups with tears.

(23) *Which of these do you consider the more important poem?*

(*a*)

Ah, Sun-flower! weary of time,
Who countest the steps of the sun;
Seeking after that sweet golden clime,
Where the traveller's journey is done;

Where the Youth pined away with desire,
And the pale Virgin shrouded in snow,
Arise from their graves, and aspire
Where my Sun-Flower wishes to go.

(*b*)

In that world we weary to attain,
    Love's furled banner floats at large unfurled;
There is no more doubt and no more pain
    In that world.

There are gems and gold and inlets pearled;
There the verdure fadeth not again;
    There no clinging tendrils droop uncurled.

Here incessant tides stir up the main,
    Stormy miry depths aloft are hurled:
There is no more sea, or storm, or stain,
    In that world.

(24) *Compare the following poems, pointing out in what respects one is better than the other:*

(*a*)

I arise from dreams of thee
In the first sweet sleep of night,
When the winds are breathing low,
And the stars are shining bright:
I arise from dreams of thee,
And a spirit in my feet
Hath led me—who knows how?
To thy chamber window, Sweet!

The wandering airs they faint
On the dark, the silent stream—
The Champak odours fail
Like sweet thoughts in a dream;
The nightingale's complaint,
It dies upon her heart;—
As I must on thine,
Oh! beloved as thou art!

Oh lift me from the grass!
I die! I faint! I fail!
Let thy love in kisses rain
On my lips and eyelids pale.
My cheek is cold and white, alas!
My heart beats loud and fast;—
Oh! press it to thine own again,
Where it will break at last.

(b)

Blame not my cheeks, though pale with love they be;
The kindly heat unto my heart is flown,
To cherish it that is dismayed by thee,
Who art so cruel and unsteadfast grown:
For nature, called for by distressed hearts,
Neglects and quite forsakes the outward parts.

But they whose cheeks with careless blood are stained,
Nurse not one spark of love within their hearts,
And, when they woo, they speak with passion feigned,
For their fat love lies in their outward parts:
But in their breasts, where love his court should hold,
Poor Cupid sits and blows his nails for cold.

(25) *Make a critical examination of the style of the following poems:*

(a)

It will not shine again,
Its sad course is done;
I have seen the last ray wane
Of the cold, bright sun.

None but me beheld him dying,
Parting with the parting day;
Wind of evening, sadly sighing,
Bore his soul from earth away.

Coldly, bleakly, dreamily
Evening died on Elbe's shore;
Winds were in the cloudy sky,
Sighing, mourning ever more.

(*b*)

The Day's grown old, the fainting Sun
Has but a little way to run,
And yet his Steeds, with all his skill,
Scarce lug the Chariot down the Hill.

With Labour spent, and Thirst opprest,
Whilst they strain hard to gain the West,
From Fetlocks hot drops melted light,
Which turns to Meteors in the Night.

The Shadows now so long do grow,
That Brambles like tall Cedars show,
Mole-hills seem Mountains, and the Ant
Appears a monstrous Elephant.

A very little little Flock
Shades thrice the ground that it would stock;
Whilst the small Stripling following them,
Appears a mighty *Polypheme*.

(26) *Compare and contrast the attitude shown to the subject in these two poems:*

(*a*)

Remember me when I am gone away,
    Gone far away into the silent land;
    When you can no more hold me by the hand,
Nor I half turn to go yet turning stay.
Remember me when no more day by day
    You tell me of our future that you plann'd:

Only remember me; you understand
It will be late to counsel then or pray.
Yet if you should forget me for a while
  And afterwards remember, do not grieve:
  For if the darkness and corruption leave
  A vestige of the thoughts that once I had,
Better by far you should forget and smile
  Than that you should remember and be sad.

(*b*)

I tell you, hopeless grief is passionless;
  That only men incredulous of despair,
  Half-taught in anguish, through the midnight air
Beat upward to God's throne in loud access
Of shrieking and reproach. Full desertness
  In souls, as countries, lieth silent-bare
  Under the blanching, vertical eye-glare
Of the absolute Heavens. Deep-hearted man, express
Grief for the Dead in silence like to death:—
  Most like a monumental statue set
In everlasting watch and moveless woe
Till itself crumble to the dust beneath.
  Touch it: the marble eyelids are not wet:
If it could weep, it could arise and go.

(27) *Point out the special qualities in thought and manner of the following poems. Which do you prefer?*

(*a*)

My tongue-tied Muse in manners holds her still,
While comments of your praise, richly compiled,
Reserve their character with golden quill,
And precious phrase by all the Muses filed.
I think good thoughts, whilst other write good words,
And, like unletter'd clerk, still cry 'Amen'
To every hymn that able spirit affords,
In polish'd form of well-refined pen.

Hearing you praised, I say ''Tis so, 'tis true',
And to the most of praise add something more;
But that is in my thought, whose love to you,
Though words come hindmost, holds his rank before.
 Then others for the breath of words respect,
 Me for my dumb thoughts, speaking in effect.

(b)

She is foremost of those that I would hear praised.
I have gone about the house, gone up and down
As a man does who has published a new book
Or a young girl dressed out in her new gown,
And though I have turned the talk by hook or crook
Until her praise should be the uppermost theme,
A woman spoke of some new tale she had read,
A man confusedly in a half dream
As though some other name ran in his head.
She is foremost of those that I would hear praised.
I will talk no more of books or the long war
But walk by the dry thorn until I have found
Some beggar sheltering from the wind, and there
Manage the talk until her name come round.
If there be rags enough he will know her name
And be well pleased remembering it, for in the old days,
Though she had young men's praise and old men's blame,
Among the poor both old and young gave her praise.

(28) *Discuss the differences between these three versions of the same passage by Keats, and try to say in what order they were written.*

(a)

As when, upon a tranced summer-night,
Those green-rob'd senators of mighty woods,
Tall oaks, branch-charmed by the earnest stars,
Dream, and so dream all night without a stir,
Save from one gradual solitary gust
Which comes upon the silence, and dies off,
As if the ebbing air had but one wave;
So came these words and went....

(*b*)

As when, upon a tranced summer-night,
Those green-rob'd senators of mighty woods,
The Oaks stand charmed by the earnest Stars:
And thus all night without a stir they rest
Save from one sudden momentary gust
Which comes upon the silence and dies off
As if the Sea of Air had but one wave:
So came these words and went....

(*c*)

As when upon a tranced summer-night
Forests, branch-charmed by the earnest stars,
Dream, and so dream all night without a noise,
Save from one gradual solitary gust,
Swelling upon the silence; dying off;
As if the ebbing air had but one wave;
So came these words and went....

(29) *Examine the following passages and say in what sense, and to what extent, the style of each is dramatic.*

(*a*)

Had it pleas'd heaven
To try me with affliction; had they rain'd
All kinds of sores and shames on my bare head,
Steep'd me in poverty to the very lips,
Given to captivity me and my utmost hopes,
I should have found in some place of my soul
A drop of patience: but, alas, to make me
The fixed figure for the time of scorn
To point his slow and moving finger at!
Yet could I bear that too; well, very well:
But there, where I have garner'd up my heart,
Where either I must live or bear no life,
The fountain from the which my current runs

Or else dries up; to be discarded thence!
Or keep it as a cistern for foul toads
To knot and gender in!

(b)

Oh, you gods,
Give me a worthy patience! Have I stood
Naked, alone, the shock of many fortunes?
Have I seen mischiefs numberless and mighty
Grow like a sea upon me? Have I taken
Danger as stern as death into my bosom,
And laugh'd upon it, made it but a mirth,
And flung it by? Do I live now like him,
Under this tyrant King, that languishing
Hears his sad bell and sees his mourners? Do I
Bear all this bravely, and must sink at length
Under a woman's falsehood?

(30) *Comment on the diction, imagery, feeling of the following poems,
making any comparisons or contrasts which seem to you relevant:*

(a)

The world is too much with us; late and soon,
Getting and spending, we lay waste our powers:
Little we see in Nature that is ours;
We have given our hearts away, a sordid boon!
This Sea that bares her bosom to the moon;
The winds that will be howling at all hours,
And are up-gathered now like sleeping flowers;
For this, for everything, we are out of tune;
It moves us not.—Great God! I'd rather be
A Pagan suckled in a creed outworn;
So might I, standing on this pleasant lea,
Have glimpses that would make me less forlorn;
Have sight of Proteus rising from the sea;
Or hear old Triton blow his wreathèd horn.

(*b*)

The world is charged with the grandeur of God.
   It will flame out, like shining from shook foil;
   It gathers to a greatness, like the ooze of oil
Crushed. Why do men then now not reck his rod?
Generations have trod, have trod, have trod;
   And all is seared with trade; bleared, smeared with toil;
   And wears man's smudge and shares man's smell: the soil
Is bare now, nor can foot feel, being shod.

And for all this, nature is never spent;
   There lives the dearest freshness deep down things;
And though the last lights off the black West went,
   Oh, morning, at the brown brink eastward, springs—
Because the Holy Ghost over the bent
   World broods with warm breast and with ah! bright wings.

(31) *Discuss the effect of the imagery in the following:*

(*a*)

How sweet the moonlight sleeps upon this bank!
Here will we sit, and let the sounds of music
Creep in our ears: soft stillness and the night
Become the touches of sweet harmony.
Sit, Jessica. Look how the floor of heaven
Is thick inlaid with patines of bright gold:
There's not the smallest orb which thou behold'st
But in his motion like an angel sings,
Still quiring to the young-eyed cherubins;
Such harmony is in immortal souls;
But whilst this muddy vesture of decay
Doth grossly close it in, we cannot hear it.

(*b*)

With how sad steps, O Moon, thou climb'st the skies!
How silently, and with how wan a face!
What, may it be that even in heav'nly place
That busy archer his sharp arrows tries!

Sure, if that long-with-love-acquainted eyes
Can judge of love, thou feel'st a lover's case,
I read it in thy looks; thy languisht grace,
To me, that feel the like, thy state descries.
Then, ev'n of fellowship, O moon, tell me,
Is constant love deem'd there but want of wit?
Are beauties there as proud as here they be?
Do they above love to be lov'd, and yet
Those lovers scorn whom that love doth possess?
Do they call virtue there ungratefulness?

(32) *Write a detailed critical comparison of these two poems, stating which you prefer and why.*

(a)

Nothing is so beautiful as spring—
When weeds, in wheels, shoot long and lovely and lush;
Thrush's eggs look little low heavens, and thrush
Through the echoing timber does so rinse and wring
The ear, it strikes like lightnings to hear him sing;
The glassy peartree leaves and blooms, they brush
The descending blue; that blue is all in a rush
With richness; the racing lambs too have fair their fling.

What is all this juice and all this joy?
A strain of the earth's sweet being in the beginning
In Eden garden.—Have, get, before it cloy,
Before it cloud, Christ, lord, and sour with sinning,
Innocent mind and Mayday in girl and boy,
Most, O maid's child, thy choice and worthy the winning.

(b)

When Spring comes back to England
    And crowns her brows with May,
Round the merry moonlit world
    She goes the greenwood way:
She throws a rose to Italy,
    A fleur-de-lys to France;
But round her regal morris-ring
    The seas of England dance

When Spring comes back to England
  And dons her robe of green,
There's many a nation garlanded,
  But England is the Queen;
She's Queen, She's Queen of all the world
  Beneath the laughing sky,
For the nations go a-Maying
  When they hear the New Year cry—

'Come over the water to England,
  My old love, my new love,
Come over the water to England
  In showers of flowery rain;
Come over the water to England,
  April, my true love,
And tell the heart of England
  The Spring is here again!'

(33) *Comment on the style, imagery and dramatic significance of the following passages, making any comparisons which you consider relevant:*

(*a*)

To be, or not to be: that is the question:
Whether 'tis nobler in the mind to suffer
The slings and arrows of outrageous fortune,
Or to take arms against a sea of troubles,
And by opposing end them. To die: to sleep:
No more; and by a sleep to say we end
The heart-ache, and the thousand natural shocks
That flesh is heir to, 'tis a consummation
Devoutly to be wish'd. To die, to sleep;
To sleep: perchance to dream: ay, there's the rub;
For in that sleep of death what dreams may come,
When we have shuffled off this mortal coil,
Must give us pause: there's the respect
That makes calamity of so long life;
For who would bear the whips and scorns of time,
The oppressor's wrong, the proud man's contumely,
The pangs of despised love, the law's delay,

The insolence of office, and the spurns
That patient merit of the unworthy takes,
When he himself might his quietus make
With a bare bodkin? who would fardels bear,
To grunt and sweat under a weary life,
But that the dread of something after death,
The undiscover'd country from whose bourn
No traveller returns, puzzles the will,
And makes us rather bear those ills we have
Than fly to others that we know not of?

(b)

Be it so, for I submit; his doom is fair,
That dust I am, and shall to dust return.
O welcome hour, whenever! Why delays
His hand to execute what his decree
Fixed on this day? Why do I overlive?
Why am I mocked with death, and lengthened out
To deathless pain? How gladly would I meet
Mortality, my sentence, and be earth
Insensible! How glad would lay me down
As in my mother's lap! There should I rest,
And sleep secure; his dreadful voice no more
Would thunder in my ears; no fear of worse
To me and my offspring would torment me
With cruel expectation. Yet one doubt
Pursues me still—lest all I cannot die,
Lest that pure breath of life, the Spirit of Man
Which God inspired, cannot together perish
With this corporeal clod. Then, in the grave,
Or in some other dismal place, who knows
But I shall die a living death? O thought
Horrid, if true! Yet why? It was but breath
Of life that sinned: what dies but what had life
And sin? The body properly hath neither.

(34) *Establish a preference for one over the other of the following poems:*

(*a*)

On Wenlock Edge the wood's in trouble;
His forest fleece the Wrekin heaves;
The gale, it plies the saplings double,
And thick on Severn snow the leaves.

'Twould blow like this through holt and hanger
When Uricon the city stood:
'Tis the old wind in the old anger,
But then it threshed another wood.

Then, 'twas before my time, the Roman
At yonder heaving hill would stare:
The blood that warms an English yeoman,
The thoughts that hurt him, they were there.

There, like the wind through woods in riot,
Through him the gale of life blew high;
The tree of man was never quiet:
Then 'twas the Roman, now 'tis I.

The gale, it plies the saplings double,
It blows so hard, 'twill soon be gone:
Today the Roman and his trouble
Are ashes under Uricon.

(*b*)

A wind is brushing down the clover,
It sweeps the tossing branches bare,
Blowing the poising kestrel over
The crumbling ramparts of the Caer.

It whirls the scattered leaves before us
Along the dusty road to home,
Once it awakened into chorus
The heart-strings in the ranks of Rome.

There by the gusty coppice border
The shrilling trumpets broke the halt,
The Roman line, the Roman order,
Swayed forwards to the blind assault.

Spearman and charioteer and bowman
Charged and were scattered into spray,
Savage and taciturn the Roman
Hewed upwards in the Roman way.

There—in the twilight—where the cattle
Are lowing home across the fields,
The beaten warriors left the battle
Dead on the clansmen's wicker shields.

The leaves whirl in the wind's riot
Beneath the Beacon's jutting spur,
Quiet are clan and chief, and quiet
Centurion and signifer.

(35) *Compare the following passages which are from early and late
versions of Tennyson's 'Œnone':*

(a)

There is a dale in Ida, lovelier
Than any in old Ionia, beautiful
With emerald slopes of sunny sward, that lean
Above the loud glenriver, which hath worn
A path thro' steepdown granite walls below
Mantled with flowering tendriltwine. In front
The cedarshadowy valleys open wide.
Far-seen, high over all the God-built wall
And many a snowycolumned range divine,
Mounted with awful sculptures,—men and Gods,
The work of Gods—bright on the dark-blue sky
The windy citadel of Ilion
Shone, like the crown of Troas. Hither came
Mournful Œnone wandering forlorn
Of Paris, once her playmate. Round her neck,
Her neck all marblewhite and marblecold,
Floated her hair or seemed to float in rest.
She, leaning on a vine-entwined stone,
Sang to the stillness, till the mountain-shadow
Sloped downward to her seat from the upper cliff.

(*b*)

There lies a vale in Ida, lovelier
Than all the valleys of Ionian hills.
The swimming vapour slopes across the glen,
Puts forth an arm, and creeps from pine to pine,
And loiters, slowly drawn. On either hand
The lawns and meadow-ledges midway down
Hang rich in flowers, and far below them roars
The long brook falling through the clov'n ravine
In cataract after cataract to the sea.
Behind the valley topmost Gargarus
Stands up and takes the morning: but in front
The gorges, opening wide apart, reveal
Troas and Ilion's column'd citadel,
The crown of Troas.
                  Hither came at noon
Mournful Œnone, wandering forlorn
Of Paris, once her playmate on the hills.
Her cheek had lost the rose, and round her neck
Floated her hair or seemed to float in rest.
She, leaning on a fragment twined with vine,
Sang to the stillness, till the mountain-shade
Sloped downward to her seat from the upper cliff.

(36) *Write a careful appreciation of these two poems:*

(*a*)

The sigh that heaves the grasses
   Whence thou wilt never rise
Is of the air that passes
   And knows not if it sighs.

The diamond tears adorning
   Thy low mound on the lea,
Those are the tears of morning
   That weeps, but not for thee.

(*b*)

A slumber did my spirit seal;
   I had no human fears:
She seemed a thing that could not feel
   The touch of earthly years.

No motion has she now, no force;
   She neither hears nor sees;
Rolled round in earth's diurnal course,
   With rocks, and stones, and trees.

(37) *Here are two versions of the same incident; state what is gained by the use of prose and verse respectively.*

(*a*)

So thus as they rode in the wood, there came a man flying all that ever he might. Wither wilt thou? said Beaumains. O lord, he said, help me, for here by in a slade are six thieves that have taken my lord, and bound him, so I am afeard lest they will slay him. Bring me hither, said Beaumains. And so they rode together until they came thereas was the knight bounden; and then he rode unto them, and struck one unto the death, and then another, and at the third stroke he slew the third thief, and then the other three fled. And he rode after them, and he overtook them; and then those three thieves turned again and assailed Beaumains hard, but at the last he slew them, and returned and unbound the knight.

slade: *valley.*

(*b*)

So till the dusk that follow'd evensong
Rode on the two, reviler and reviled;
Then after one long slope was mounted, saw
Bowl-shaped, thro' tops of many thousand pines
A gloomy-gladed hollow slowly sink
To westward—in the deeps whereof a mere,
Round as the red eye of an Eagle-owl,
Under the half-dead sunset glared; and shouts
Ascended, and there brake a servingman

Flying from out of the black wood, and crying,
'They have bound my lord to cast him in the mere.'
Then Gareth, 'Bound am I to right the wrong'd,
But straitlier bound am I to bide with thee.'
And when the damsel spake contemptuously,
'Lead, and I follow', Gareth cried again,
'Follow, I lead!' so down among the pines
He plunged; and there, blackshadow'd nigh the mere,
And mid-thigh-deep in bulrushes and reed,
Saw six tall men haling a seventh along,
A stone about his neck to drown him in it.
Three with good blows he quieted, but three
Fled thro' the pines; and Gareth loosed the stone
From off his neck, then in the mere beside
Tumbled it; oilily bubbled up the mere.
Last, Gareth loosed his bonds and on free feet
Set him, a stalwart Baron, Arthur's friend.

(38) *Establish a preference for one of these poems:*

(*a*)

'Twas at the season when the Earth upsprings
From slumber; as a spherèd angel's child,
Shadowing its eyes with green and golden wings,
    Stands up before its mother bright and mild,
Of whose soft voice the air expectant seems—
So stood before the sun, which shone and smiled
    To see it ride thus joyous from its dreams,
The fresh and radiant Earth. The hoary grove
Waxed green, and flowers burst forth like starry beams;
    The grass in the warm sun did start and move,
And sea-buds burst under the waves serene:—
How many a one, though none be near to love,
    Loves then the shade of his own soul, half seen
In any mirror—or the spring's young minions,
The wingèd leaves amid the copses green:
    How many a spirit then puts on the pinions
Of fancy, and outstrips the lagging blast,
And his own steps, and over wide dominions

Sweeps in his dream-drawn chariot, far and fast,
More fleet than storms. The wide world shrinks below,
When winter and despondency are past.

(b)

The glory of the beauty of the morning,—
The cuckoo crying over the untouched dew;
The blackbird that has found it, and the dove
That tempts me on to something sweeter than love;
White clouds ranged even and fair as new-mown hay;
The heat, the stir, the sublime vacancy
Of sky and meadow and forest and my own heart:—
The glory invites me, yet it leaves me scorning
All I can ever do, all I can be,
Beside the lovely of motion, shape, and hue,
The happiness I fancy fit to dwell
In beauty's presence. Shall I now this day
Begin to seek as far as heaven, as hell,
Wisdom or strength to match this beauty, start
And tread the pale dust pitted with small dark drops,
In hope to find whatever it is I seek,
Hearkening to short-lived happy-seeming things
That we know naught of, in the hazel copse?
Or must I be content with discontent
As larks and swallows are perhaps with wings?
And shall I ask at the day's end once more
What beauty is, and what I can have meant
By happiness? And shall I let all go,
Glad, weary, or both? Or shall I perhaps know
That I was happy oft and oft before,
Awhile forgetting how I am fast pent,
How dreary-swift, with naught to travel to,
Is Time? I cannot bite the day to the core.

(39) *Comment on the rhythm and structure of these sonnets. Show in what ways each poem is effective.*

(*a*)

Avenge, O Lord! Thy slaughter'd saints, whose bones
Lie scatter'd on the Alpine mountains cold;
Even them who kept Thy truth so pure of old
When all our fathers worshipt stocks and stones
Forget not: In Thy book record their groans
Who were thy sheep, and in their ancient fold
Slain by the bloody Piemontese, that roll'd
Mother with infant down the rocks. Their moans
The vales redoubled to the hills, and they
To Heaven. Their martyr'd blood and ashes sow
O'er all the Italian fields, where still doth sway
The triple Tyrant, that from these may grow
A hundred-fold, who, having learnt Thy way,
Early may fly the Babylonian woe.

(*b*)

This is my play's last scene; here heavens appoint
My pilgrimage's last mile; and my race
Idly, yet quickly run, hath this last pace;
My span's last inch, my minute's latest point;
And gluttonous Death will instantly unjoint
My body and soul, and I shall sleep a space;
But my ever-waking part shall see that face,
Whose fear already shakes my every joint.
Then, as my soul to heaven, her first seat, takes flight,
And earth-borne body in the earth shall dwell,
So fall my sins, that all may have their right,
To where they're bred and would press me to hell.
Impute me righteous, thus purged of evil,
For thus I leave the world, the flesh, the devil.

(*c*)

But be contented: when that fell arrest
Without all bail shall carry me away,
My life hath in this line some interest,

Which for memorial still with thee shall stay.
When thou reviewest this, thou dost review
The very part was consecrate to thee:
The earth can have but earth, which is his due;
My spirit is thine, the better part of me:
So then thou hast but lost the dregs of life,
The prey of worms, my body being dead;
The coward conquest of a wretch's knife,
Too base of thee to be remembered.
The worth of that is that which it contains,
And that is this, and this with thee remains.

(40) *Compare and contrast the two following poems paying particular
attention to their versification, diction, imagery and feeling:*

(*a*)

I caught this morning morning's minion, king-
   dom of daylight's dauphin, dapple-dawn-drawn Falcon, in his
      riding
Of the rolling level underneath him steady air, and striding
High there, how he rung upon the rein of a wimpling wing
In his ecstasy! then off, off forth on swing,
   As a skate's heel sweeps smooth on a bow-bend: the hurl and
      gliding
   Rebuffed the big wind. My heart in hiding
Stirred for a bird,—the achieve of, the mastery of the thing!

Brute beauty and valour and act, oh, air, pride, plume, here
   Buckle! AND the fire that breaks from thee then, a billion
Times told lovelier, more dangerous, O my chevalier!
   No wonder of it: shéer plód makes plough down sillion
Shine, and blue-bleak embers, ah my dear,
   Fall, gall themselves, and gash gold-vermilion.

(*b*)

The hawk slipt out of the pine, and rose in the sunlit air:
Steady and still he poised; his shadow slept on the grass:
And the bird's song sickened and sank: she cowered with furtive
   stare,

Dumb, till the quivering dimness should flicker and shift and pass.
Suddenly down he dropped: she heard the hiss of his wing,
Fled with a scream of terror: oh, would she had dared to rest!
For the hawk at eve was full, and there was no bird to sing,
And over the heather drifted the down from a bleeding breast.

(41) *Compare these two lyrical poems, and say which you find the more satisfying:*

(a)

If I could shut the gate against my thoughts
    And keep out sorrow from this room within,
Or memory could cancel all the notes
    Of my misdeeds, and I unthink my sin;
How free, how clear, how clean my soul should lie,
Discharged of such a loathsome company!

Or were there other rooms without my heart
    That did not to my conscience join so near,
Where I might lodge the thoughts of sin apart
    That I might not their clam'rous crying hear;
What peace, what joy, what ease should I possess,
Freed from their horrors that my soul oppress!

But, O my Saviour, who my refuge art,
    Let thy dear mercies stand 'twixt them and me,
And be the wall to separate my heart
    So that I may at length repose me free;
That peace, and joy, and rest may be within,
And I remain divided from my sin.

(b)

When I sit reading all alone that secret book
Wherein I sigh to look,
How many spots there be
I wish I could not see,
Or from myself might flee!

Mine eyes for refuge then with zeal befix the skies,
My tears do cloud those eyes,
My sighs do blow them dry;
And yet I live to die
Myself I cannot fly.

Heaven, I implore, that knows my fault, what shall I do?
To Hell I dare not go;
The world first made me rue,
My self my griefs renew:
To whom then shall I sue?

Alas, my soul doth faint to draw this doubtful breath:
Is there no hope in death?
O yes, death ends my woes,
Death me from me will loose;
My self am all my foes.

(42) *How do the following poems differ in their treatment of the
subject? Which poem do you prefer?*

(*a*)

Fair pledges of a fruitful tree,
   Why do ye fall so fast?
   Your date is not so past;
But you may stay yet here a while,
   To blush and gently smile;
     And go at last.

What, were ye born to be
   An hour or half's delight;
   And so to bid goodnight?
'Twas pity Nature brought ye forth
   Merely to show your worth,
     And lose you quite.

But you are lovely leaves, where we
   May read how soon things have
   Their end, though ne'er so brave:
And after they have shown their pride,
   Like you a while: they glide
     Into the grave.

(*b*)

Little think'st thou, poor flower,
Whom I have watched six or seven days,
And seen thy birth, and seen what every hour
Gave to thy growth, thee to this height to raise,
And now dost laugh and triumph on this bough,
   Little think'st thou
That it will freeze anon, and that I shall
Tomorrow find thee fallen, or not at all.

Little think'st thou poor heart
That labour'st yet to nestle thee,
And think'st by hovering here to get a part
In a forbidden or forbidding tree,
And hop'st her stiffness by long siege to bow:
   Little think'st thou,
That thou tomorrow, ere that sun doth wake,
Must with this sun, and me a journey take.

(43) *Here are two drafts of the same poem. Compare them in some detail, and say which you consider the later version.*

(*a*)

Old Yew, which graspest at the stones
   That name the under-lying dead,
   Thy fibres net the dreamless head,
Thy roots are wrapt about the bones.

The seasons bring the flower again,
   And bring the firstling to the flock;
   And in the dusk of thee, the clock
Beats out the little lives of men.

O not for thee the glow, the bloom,
   Who changest not in any gale,
   Nor branding summer suns avail
To touch thy thousand years of gloom:

And gazing on thee, sullen tree,
   Sick for thy sullen hardihood,
   I seem to fail from out my blood
And grow incorporate into thee.

(b)

Old warder of these buried bones,
   And answering now my random stroke
   With fruitful cloud and living smoke,
Dark yew, that graspest at the stones

And dippest towards the dreamless head,
   To thee too comes the golden hour
   When flower is feeling after flower;
But sorrow—fixt upon the dead,

And darkening the dark graves of men,—
   What whisper'd from her lying lips?
   Thy gloom is kindled at the tips,
And passes into gloom again.

(44) *Which of the two following invocations of disorder do you consider
to be the more effective?*

(a)

Now bind my brows with iron; and approach
The ragged'st hour that time and spite dare bring
To frown upon the enraged Northumberland!
Let heaven kiss earth! now let not Nature's hand
Keep the wild flood confined! let order die!
And let this world no longer be a stage
To feed contention in a lingering act;
But let one spirit of the first-born Cain
Reign in all bosoms, that, each heart being set
On bloody courses, the rude scene may end,
And darkness be the burier of the dead!

(b)

I conjure you, by that which you profess,
Howe'er you come to know it, answer me:
Though you untie the winds, and let them fight

Against the churches; though the yesty-waves
Confound and swallow navigation up;
Though bladed corn be lodg'd, and trees blown down;
Though castles topple on their warders' heads;
Though palaces, and pyramids, do slope
Their heads to their foundations; though the treasure
Of nature's germens tumble all together,
Even till destruction sicken, answer me
To what I ask you.

(45) *Comment on the style, imagery, and dramatic significance of the following passages:*

(a)

Time hath, my lord, a wallet at his back
Wherein he puts alms for oblivion,
A great-sized monster of ingratitudes:
Those scraps are good deeds past, which are devour'd
As fast as they are made, forgot as soon
As done: perseverance, dear my lord,
Keeps honour bright: to have done, is to hang
Quite out of fashion, like a rusty mail
In monumental mockery. Take the instant way;
For honour travels in a strait so narrow,
Where one but goes abreast: keep then the path;
For emulation hath a thousand sons,
That one by one pursue: if you give way,
Or hedge aside from the direct forthright,
Like to an enter'd tide they all rush by
And leave you hindmost:
Or, like a gallant horse fall'n in first rank,
Lie there for pavement to the abject rear,
O'er-run and trampled on: then what they do in present,
Though less than yours in past, must o'ertop yours;
For time is like a fashionable host
That slightly shakes his parting guest by the hand,
And with his arms outstretch'd, as he would fly,
Grasps in the comer: welcome ever smiles,
And farewell goes out sighing.

(*b*)

These God-like Vertues wherefore dost thou hide?
Affecting private life, or more obscure
In savage Wilderness, wherefore deprive
All Earth her wonder at thy acts, thy self
The fame and glory, glory the reward
That sole excites to high attempts the flame
Of most erected Spirits, most temper'd pure
Ætherial, who all pleasures else despise,
All treasures and all gain esteem as dross,
And dignities and powers all but the highest?
Thy years are ripe, and over-ripe, the Son
Of Macedonian Philip had e're these
Won Asia and the Throne of Cyrus held
At his dispose, young Scipio had brought down
The Carthaginian pride, young Pompey quell'd
The Pontic King and in triumph had rode.
Yet years, and to ripe years judgment mature,
Quench not the thirst of glory, but augment.
Great Julius, whom now all the world admires,
The more he grew in years, the more inflam'd
With glory, wept that he had liv'd so long
Inglorious: but thou yet art not too late.

(46) *Point out the special qualities in thought and manner of these two poems:*

(*a*)

Come not, when I am dead,
   To drop thy foolish tears upon my grave,
To trample round my fallen head,
   And vex the unhappy dust thou wouldst not save.
There let the wind sweep and the plover cry;
   But thou, go by.

Child if it were thine error or thy crime
   I care no longer, being all unblest:

Wed whom thou wilt, but I am sick of Time,
  And I desire to rest.
Pass on, weak heart, and leave me where I lie:
  Go by, go by.

(b)

No longer mourn for me when I am dead
Than you shall hear the surly sullen bell
Give warning to the world that I am fled
From this vile world, with vilest worms to dwell;
Nay, if you read this line, remember not
The hand that writ it; for I love you so,
That I in your sweet thoughts would be forgot,
If thinking on me then should make you woe.
O, if, I say, you look upon this verse
When I perhaps compounded am with clay,
Do not so much as my poor name rehearse,
But let your love even with my life decay;
    Lest the wise world should look into your moan,
    And mock you with me after I am gone.

(47) *Which of these is the more effective poem?*

(a)

The sun that in Breadalbane's lake doth fall
Was melting to the sea down golden Tay,
When a cry came along the peopled way,
'Sebastopol is ours!' From that wild call
I turned, and leaning on a time-worn wall
Quaint with the touch of many an ancient day,
The mappèd mould and mildewed marquetry
Knew with my focused soul; which bent down all
Its sense, power, passion, to the sole regard
Of each green minim, as it were but born
To that one use. I strode home stern and hard;
In my hot hands I laid my throbbing head,
And all the living world and all the dead
Began a march which did not end at morn.

(b)

The wind flapped loose, the wind was still,
Shaken out dead from tree and hill:
I had walked on at the wind's will,—
I sat now for the wind was still.

Between my knees my forehead was,—
My lips, drawn in, said not Alas!
My hair was over in the grass,
My naked ears heard the day pass.

My eyes, wide open, had the run
Of some ten weeds to fix upon;
Among those few out of the sun:
The woodspurge flowered, three cups in one.

From perfect grief there need not be
Wisdom or even memory:
One thing then learnt remains to me,—
The woodspurge has a cup of three.

(48) *Either compare the following poems, or write a detailed criticism of one of them:*

(a)

Long expected one-and-twenty,
    Ling'ring year, at length is flown;
Pride and pleasure, pomp and plenty,
    Great Sir John, are now your own.

Loosen'd from the minor's tether,
    Free to mortgage or to sell;
Wild as wind, and light as feather,
    Bid the sons of thrift farewell.

Call the Betsies, Kates, and Jennies,
    All the names that banish care;
Lavish of your grandsire's guineas,
    Show the spirit of an heir.

All that prey on vice or folly
　Joy to see their quarry fly:
There the gamester, light and jolly,
　There the lender, grave and sly.

Wealth, my lad, was made to wander,
　Let it wander as it will;
Call the jockey, call the pander,
　Bid them come and take their fill.

When the bonny blade carouses,
　Pockets full, and spirits high—
What are acres? what are houses?
　Only dirt or wet or dry.

Should the guardian friend, or mother
　Tell the woes of wilful waste;
Scorn their counsel, scorn their pother,
　You can hang or drown at last.

(b)

Shot? so quick, so clean an ending?
　Oh that was right, lad, that was brave:
Yours was not an ill for mending,
　'Twas best to take it to the grave.

Oh you had forethought, you could reason,
　And saw your road and where it led,
And early wise and brave in season
　Put the pistol to your head.

Oh soon, and better so than later
　After long disgrace and scorn,
You shot dead the household traitor,
　The soul that should not have been born.

Right you guessed the rising morrow
　And scorned to tread the mire you must:
Dust's your wages, son of sorrow,
　But men may come to worse than dust.

Souls undone, undoing others,—
    Long time since the tale began.
You would not live to wrong your brothers:
    Oh lad, you died as fits a man.

Now to your grave shall friend and stranger
    With ruth and some with envy come:
Undishonoured, clear of danger,
    Clean of guilt, pass hence and home.

Turn safe to rest, no dreams, no waking;
    And here, man, here's the wreath I've made:
'Tis not a gift that's worth the taking,
    But wear it and it will not fade.

(49) *Contrast the personalities shown in these two poems:*

(*a*)

When I consider how my light is spent,
    Ere half my days in this dark world and wide,
    And that one Talent which is death to hide
Lodged with me useless, though my Soul more bent
To serve therewith my Maker and present
    My true account lest he returning chide,—
    Doth God exact day-labour, light denied?
I fondly ask; But Patience, to prevent
That murmur, soon replies: God doth not need
    Either man's work or his own gifts; who best
        Bear his mild yoke, they serve him best; his State
Is kingly. Thousands at his bidding speed
    And post o'er Land and Ocean without rest.
        They also serve who only stand and wait.

(*b*)

When I have fears that I may cease to be
    Before my pen has gleaned my teeming brain,
Before high-piled books, in charact'ry,
    Hold like rich garners the full-ripened grain;
When I behold, upon the night's starred face,
    Huge cloudy symbols of a high romance,

And think that I may never live to trace
   Their shadows with the magic hand of chance;
And when I feel, frail creature of an hour,
   That I shall never look upon thee more,
Never have relish in the faery power
   Of unreflecting love!—then on the shore
Of the wide world I stand alone, and think
Till Love and Fame to nothingness do sink.

(50) *Compare the following two poems as to subject matter and treatment:*

(*a*)

    Proud Maisie is in the wood,
      Walking so early;
    Sweet Robin sits on the bush,
      Singing so rarely.

    'Tell me, thou bonny bird,
      When shall I marry me?'
    'When six braw gentlemen
      Kirkward shall carry ye.'

    'Who makes the bridal bed,
      Birdie, say truly?'
    'The grey-headed sexton
      That delves the grave duly.

    'The glow-worm o'er grave and stone
      Shall light thee steady.
    The owl from the steeple sing,
      "Welcome, proud lady."'

(*b*)

Who said, 'Peacock Pie'?
   The old King to the sparrow:
Who said, 'Crops are ripe'?
   Rust to the harrow:
Who said, 'Where sleeps she now?
   Where rests she now her head,
Bathed in eve's loveliness'?
   That's what I said.

Who said, 'Ay, mum's the word'?
   Sexton to willow:
Who said, 'Green dust for dreams,
   Moss for a pillow'?
Who said, 'All Time's delight
   Hath she for narrow bed;
Life's troubled bubble broken'?—
   That's what I said.

(51) *Compare these versions of a traditional ballad, and say which one you prefer:*

(*a*)

There were three rauens sat on a tree,
They were as black as they might be.

The one of them said to his mate,
'Where shall we our breakfast take?'

'Down in yonder greene field,
There lies a knight slain vnder his shield.

'His hounds they lie downe at his feete,
So well they can their master keepe.

'His haukes they flie so eagerly,
There's no fowle dare him come nie.'

Downe there comes a fallow doe,
As great with young as she might goe.

She lift vp his bloudy hed,
And kist the wounds that were so red.

She got him vp vpon her backe,
And carried him to earthen lake.

She buried him before the prime,
She was dead herselfe ere euen-song time.

God send euery gentleman,
Such haukes, such hounds, and such a leman.

(*b*)

As I was walking all alane,
I heard twa corbies making a mane;
The tane unto the t'other did say,
'Where sall we gang to dine to-day?'

'In behint yon auld fail dyke,
I wot there lies a new-slain knight;
And naebody kens that he lies there,
But his hawk, his hound, and his lady fair.

'His hound is to the hunting gane,
His hawk to fetch the wild-fowl hame,
His lady's ta'en another mate,
So we may make our dinner sweet.

'Ye'll sit on his white hause-bane,
And I'll pike out his bonny blue een;
Wi' ae lock o' his gowden hair
We'll theek our nest when it grows bare.

'Mony a one for him makes mane,
But nane sall ken whare he is gane;
Oer his white banes, when they are bare
The wind sall blaw for evermair.'

(52) *Which of these two is the better poem?*

(*a*)

Love bade me welcome; yet my soul drew back,
    Guilty of dust and sin.
But quick-eyed Love, observing me grow slack
    From my first entrance in,
Drew nearer to me, sweetly questioning
    If I lack'd anything.

'A guest', I answer'd, 'worthy to be here':
    Love said, 'You shall be he.'

'I, the unkind, ungrateful? Ah, my dear,
  I cannot look on Thee.'
Love took my hand and smiling did reply,
  'Who made the eyes but I?'

'Truth, Lord; but I have marr'd them: let my shame
  Go where it doth deserve.'
'And you know not', says Love, 'Who bore the blame?'
  'My dear, then will I serve.'
 You must sit down', says Love, 'and taste my meat.'
  So I did sit and eat.

                    (*b*)

        'Lord, in Thy Courts
          Are seats so green bestow'd,
        As there resorts
          Along the dusty road
A cavalcade,—King, Bishop, Knight, and Judge:
And though I toil behind and meanly trudge,
Let me, too, lie upon that pleasant sward,
          For I am weary, Lord.

        'Christ, at thy board
          Are wines and dishes drest
        That do afford
          Contentment to the best.
And though with poverty my bed hath been
These many years and my refreshment lean,
With plenty now at last my soul acquaint,
          Dear Master, for I faint!'

        But through the grille,
          'Where is thy Robe?' said He,
        'Wouldst eat thy fill,
          Yet shirk civility?'
'My Robe, alas! There was a little child
That shivered by the road'—Swiftly God smiled;
'I was that Child,' said He, and raised the pin;
          'Dear friend, enter thou in!'

(53) *How do the following passages differ in their treatment of the subject?*

(*a*)

Enquirer, cease, petitions yet remain,
Which heav'n may hear, nor deem religion vain.
Still raise for good the supplicating voice,
But leave to heav'n the measure and the choice.
Safe in his pow'r, whose eyes discern afar
The secret ambush of a specious prayer.
Implore his aid, in his decisions rest,
Secure whate'er he gives, he gives the best.

(*b*)

Therefore to whom turn I but to Thee, the ineffable Name?
  Builder and maker, Thou, of houses not made with hands!
What, have fear of change from Thee who art ever the same?
  Doubt that Thy power can fill the heart that Thy power expands?
There shall never be one lost good! What was, shall live as before;
  The evil is null, is nought, is silence implying sound;
What was good, shall be good, with, for evil, so much good more;
  On the earth the broken arcs; in the heaven, a perfect round.

(54) *Compare the following poems. What attitude to their subject do the writers show? Which poem do you prefer?*

(*a*)

Because I could not stop for Death,
He kindly stopped for me;
The carriage held but just ourselves
And Immortality.

We slowly drove, he knew no haste,
And I had put away
My labour and my leisure too,
For his civility.

We passed the school where children played,
Their lessons scarcely done;
We passed the fields of gazing grain,
We passed the setting sun.

196

We paused before a house that seemed
A swelling on the ground;
The roof was scarcely visible,
The cornice but a mound.

Since then 'tis centuries; but each
Feels shorter than the day
I first surmised the horses' heads
Were toward eternity.

(*b*)

Good-bye, Winter
The days are getting longer,
The tea-leaf in the teacup
Is herald of a stranger.

Will he bring me business
Or will he bring me gladness
Or will he come for cure
Of his own sickness?

With a pedlar's burden
Walking up the garden
Will he come to beg
Or will he come to bargain?

Will he come to pester,
To cringe or to bluster,
A promise in his palm
Or a gun in his holster?

Will his name be John
Or will his name be Jonah,
Crying to repent
On the island of Iona?

Will his name be Jason
Looking for a seaman
Or a mad crusader
Without rhyme or reason?

What will be his message—
War or work or marriage?
News as new as dawn
Or an old adage?

Will he give a champion
Answer to my question
Or will his words be dark
And his ways evasion?

Will his name be love
And all his talk be crazy
Or will his name be Death
And his message easy?

(55) *Compare the following, and say which you consider to be the more important poem:*

(a)

The rose was sick and smiling died;
And, being to be sanctified,
About the bed there sighing stood
The sweet and flowery sisterhood:
Some hung the head, while some did bring,
To wash her, water from the spring;
Some laid her forth, while others wept,
But all a solemn fast there kept:
The holy sisters, some among,
The sacred dirge and trental sung.
But ah! what sweets smelt everywhere,
As Heaven had spent all perfumes there.
At last, when prayers for the dead
And rites were all accomplished,
They, weeping, spread a lawny loom,
And closed her up as in a tomb.

(b)

O Rose, thou art sick!
The invisible worm
That flies in the night,
In the howling storm,

Has found out thy bed
Of crimson joy,
And his dark secret love
Does thy life destroy.

(56) *Discuss the meaning, and give your critical opinion of the quality of these two poems:*

(*a*)

Batter my heart, three-person'd God; for, you
As yet but knock, breathe, shine, and seek to mend;
That I may rise, and stand, o'erthrow me, and bend
Your force, to break, blow, burn and make me new.
I, like an usurped town, to another due,
Labour to admit you, but O, to no end.
Reason, your viceroy in me, me should defend,
But is captiv'd, and proves weak or untrue.
Yet dearly I love you, and would be loved fain,
But am betroth'd unto your enemy:
Divorce me, untie, or break that knot again,
Take me to you, imprison me, for I
Except you enthrall me, never shall be free,
Nor ever chaste, except you ravish me.

(*b*)

The Lord will happiness divine
    On contrite hearts bestow:
Then tell me, gracious God, is mine
    A contrite heart, or no?

I hear, but seem to hear in vain,
    Insensible as steel;
If ought is felt, 'tis only pain,
    To feel I cannot feel.

I sometimes think myself inclin'd
    To love thee, if I could;
But often feel another mind,
    Averse to all that's good.

My best desires are faint and few,
  I fain would strive for more;
But when I cry, 'My strength renew',
  Seem weaker than before.

Thy saints are comforted I know,
  And love thy house of pray'r;
I therefore go where others go,
  But find no comfort there.

Oh make this heart rejoice, or ache;
  Decide this doubt for me;
And if it be not broken, break,
  And heal it, if it be.

(57) *Discuss the characteristics and peculiarities of the following two poems:*

(*a*)

You should be done with blossoming by now.
Yet here are leaves closer than any bough
That welcomes ivy. True, you were a tree
And stood with others in a marching line,
Less regular than this, of spruce and pine,
And boasted branches rather than a trunk.
This is your final winter, all arms shrunk
To one cross-bar bearing haphazardly
Four rusty strands. You cannot hope to feel
The electric sap run through those veins of steel.
The birds know this; the birds have hoodwinked you,
Crowding about you as they used to do.
The rainy robins huddled on your wire
And those black birds with shoulders dipped in fire
Have made you dream these vines; these tendrils are
A last despair in green, familiar
To derelicts of earth as well as sea.
Do not believe them, there is mockery
In their cool little jets of song. They know
What everyone but you learned long ago:
The stream of stories humming through your head
Is not your own. You dream. But you are dead.

(b)

Here come the line-gang pioneering by.
They throw a forest down less cut than broken.
They plant dead trees for living, and the dead
They string together with a living thread.
They string an instrument against the sky
Wherein words, whether beaten out or spoken,
Will run as hushed as when they were a thought.
But in no hush they string it: they go past
With shouts afar to pull the cable taut,
To hold it hard until they make it fast,
To ease away—they have it. With a laugh
And oaths of towns that set the wild at naught,
They bring the telephone and the telegraph.

(58) *Comment on the following passages, and say which of the two is
the more convincing:*

(a)

...Most souls, 'tis true, but peep out once an age,
Dull, sullen prisoners in the body's cage;
Dim lights of life, that burn a length of years,
Useless, unseen, as lamps in sepulchres;
Like eastern kings, a lazy state they keep,
And close confined to their own palace, sleep....
Yet shall thy grave with rising flowers be dressed,
And the green turf lie lightly on thy breast:
There shall the morn her earliest tears bestow,
There the first roses of the year shall blow;
While angels with their silver wings o'ershade
The ground, now sacred by thy relics made.
So peaceful rests, without a stone, a name,
What once had beauty, titles, wealth and fame.
How loved, how honoured once, avails thee not
To whom related, or by whom begot;
A heap of dust alone remains of thee:
'Tis all thou art, and all the proud shall be!
Poets themselves must fall, like those they sung,
Deaf the praised ear and mute the tuneful tongue.

Ev'n he whose soul now melts in mournful lays
Shall shortly want the generous tear he pays;
Then from his closing eyes thy form shall part,
And the last pang shall tear thee from his heart:
Life's idle business at one gasp be o'er,
The Muse forgot, and thou beloved no more!

(*b*)

Sleep on, my Love, in thy cold bed,
Never to be disquieted!
My last good night! Thou wilt not wake
Till I thy fate shall overtake:
Till age or grief or sickness must
Marry my body to that dust
It so much loves; and fill the room
My heart keeps empty in thy tomb.
Stay for me there; I will not fail
To meet thee in that hollow vale;
And think not much of my delay;
I am already on the way,
And follow thee with all the speed
Desire can make or sorrows breed.
Each minute is a short degree,
And ev'ry hour a step towards thee.
At night, when I betake to rest,
Next morn I rise nearer my West
Of Life, almost by eight hours' sail
Than when sleep breathed his drowsy gale....
The thought of this bids me go on,
And wait my dissolution
With hope and comfort. Dear (forgive
The crime) I am content to live
Divided, with but half a heart,
Till we shall meet and never part.

(59) *Point out the special qualities in thought and manner of the following passages:*

(a)

Happy those early days, when I
Shined in my Angel-infancy!
Before I understood this place
Appointed for my second race,
Or taught my soul to fancy aught
But a white celestial thought;
When yet I had not walked above
A mile or two from my first Love,
And looking back—at that short space—
Could see a glimpse of His bright face:
When on some gilded cloud, or flower,
My gazing soul would dwell an hour,
And in those weaker glories spy
Some shadows of eternity;
Before I taught my tongue to wound
My Conscience with a sinful sound,
Or had the black art to dispense
A several sin to every sense,
But felt through all this fleshly dress
Bright shoots of everlastingness.

O how I long to travel back,
And tread again that ancient track!
That I might once more reach that plain,
Where first I left my glorious train;
From whence th' enlightened spirit sees
That shady City of Palm trees.
But ah! my soul with too much stay
Is drunk, and staggers in the way!
Some men a forward motion love,
But I by backward steps would move;
And when this dust falls to the urn,
In that state I came, return.

(*b*)

The thought of our past years in me doth breed
Perpetual benediction: not indeed
For that which is most worthy to be blest,
Delight and liberty, the simple creed
Of childhood, whether busy or at rest,
With new-fledged hope still fluttering in his breast:
    Not for these I raise
    The song of thanks and praise;
But for those obstinate questionings
Of sense and outward things,
Fallings from us, vanishings,
Blank misgivings of a creature
Moving about in worlds not realised,
High instincts, before which our mortal nature
Did tremble like a guilty thing surprised:
    But for those first affections,
    Those shadowy recollections,
      Which, be they what they may,
Are yet the fountain-light of all our day,
Are yet a master-light of all our seeing;
    Uphold us, cherish, and have power to make
Our noisy years seem moments in the being
    Of the eternal silence: truths that wake,
      To perish never;
Which neither listlessness, nor mad endeavour,
    Nor man nor boy
Nor all that is at enmity with joy,
Can utterly abolish or destroy!
    Hence in a season of calm weather
      Though inland far we be,
      Our souls have sight of that immortal sea
    Which brought us hither;
    Can in a moment travel thither,
And see the children sport upon the shore,
And hear the mighty waters rolling evermore.

(60) *Explain clearly the similarities and differences you find in the thought in these poems, and comment on their poetic merits:*

(*a*)

Brave flowers, that I could gallant it like you
    And be as little vaine!
You come abroad, and make a harmlesse shew,
    And to your bedds of Earth againe;
You are not proud, you know your birth
For your Embroiderd garments are from Earth.

You doe obey your moneths, and times, but I
    Would have it ever Springe,
My fate would know noe Winter, never dye,
    Nor thinke of such a thing;
Oh that I could my bed of Earth but view
And Smile, and looke as chearefully as you:

Oh teach me to see Death, and not to feare,
    But rather to take truce;
How often have I seene you at a Beere,
    And there looke fresh and spruce;
You fragrant flowers then teach me that my breath
Like yours may sweeten, and perfume my death.

(*b*)

I made a posie, while the day ran by;
Here will I smell my remnant out, and tie
    My life within this band.
But time did beckon to the flowers, and they
By noon most cunningly did steal away
    And wither'd in my hand.

My hand was next to them, and then my heart:
I took, without more thinking, in good part
    Time's gentle admonition:
Who did so sweetly death's sad taste convey,
Making my minde to smell my fatall day,
    Yet sug'ring the suspicion.

Farewell, deare flowers, sweetly your time ye spent,
Fit, while ye liv'd, for smell or ornament,
    And after death for cures.
I follow straight without complaints or grief,
Since, if my scent be good, I care not if
    It be as short as yours.

APPENDIX

TEXTS OF THE POEMS OF SECTION IV

HOMER, *Iliad* VIII, 542-61

ὣς Ἕκτωρ ἀγόρευ', ἐπὶ δὲ Τρῶες κελάδησαν.
οἱ δ' ἵππους μὲν λῦσαν ὑπὸ ζυγοῦ ἱδρώοντας,
δῆσαν δ' ἱμάντεσσι παρ' ἅρμασιν οἷσιν ἕκαστος·
ἐκ πόλιος δ' ἄξοντο βόας καὶ ἴφια μῆλα
καρπαλίμως, οἶνον δὲ μελίφρονα οἰνίζοντο,
σῖτόν τ' ἐκ μεγάρων, ἐπὶ δὲ ξύλα πολλὰ λέγοντο.
κνίσην δ' ἐκ πεδίου ἄνεμοι φέρον οὐρανὸν εἴσω.
   Οἱ δὲ μέγα φρονέοντες ἐπὶ πτολέμοιο γεφύρας
ἥατο παννύχιοι, πυρὰ δέ σφισι καίετο πολλά.
ὡς δ' ὅτ' ἐν οὐρανῷ ἄστρα φαεινὴν ἀμφὶ σελήνην
φαίνετ' ἀριπρεπέα, ὅτε τ' ἔπλετο νήνεμος αἰθήρ·
ἔκ τ' ἔφανεν πᾶσαι σκοπιαὶ καὶ πρώονες ἄκροι
καὶ νάπαι· οὐρανόθεν δ' ἄρ' ὑπερράγη ἄσπετος αἰθήρ,
πάντα δὲ εἴδεται ἄστρα, γέγηθε δέ τε φρένα ποιμήν·
τόσσα μεσηγὺ νεῶν ἠδὲ Ξάνθοιο ῥοάων
Τρώων καιόντων πυρὰ φαίνετο Ἰλιόθι πρό.
χίλι' ἄρ' ἐν πεδίῳ πυρὰ καίετο, πὰρ δε ἑκάστῳ
ἥατο πεντήκοντα σέλαι πυρὸς αἰθομένοιο.
ἵπποι δὲ κρῖ λευκὸν ἐρεπτόμενοι καὶ ὀλύρας
ἑσταότες παρ' ὄχεσφιν ἐΰθρονον Ἠῶ μίμνον.

HOMER, *Odyssey* XXIV, 1-14

Ἑρμῆς δὲ ψυχὰς Κυλλήνιος ἐξεκαλεῖτο
ἀνδρῶν μνηστήρων· ἔχε δὲ ῥάβδον μετὰ χερσὶ
καλὴν χρυσείην, τῇ τ' ἀνδρῶν ὄμματα θέλγει
ὧν ἐθέλει, τοὺς δ' αὖτε καὶ ὑπνώοντας ἐγείρει·
τῇ ῥ' ἄγε κινήσας, ταὶ δὲ τρίζουσαι ἕποντο.
ὡς δ' ὅτε νυκτερίδες μυχῷ ἄντρου θεσπεσίοιο

τρίζουσαι ποτέονται, ἐπεί κέ τις ἀποπέσῃσιν
ὁρμαθοῦ ἐκ πέτρης, ἀνά τ' ἀλλήλῃσιν ἔχονται,
ὣς αἱ τετριγυῖαι ἅμ' ἤϊσαν· ἄρχε δ' ἄρα σφιν
Ἑρμείας ἀκάκητα κατ' εὐρώεντα κέλευθα.
πὰρ δ' ἴσαν Ὠκεανοῦ τε ῥοὰς καὶ Λευκάδα πέτρην,
ἠδὲ παρ' Ἠελίοιο πύλας καὶ δῆμον ὀνείρων
ἤϊσαν· αἶψα δ' ἵκοντο κατ' ἀσφοδελὸν λειμῶνα,
ἔνθα τε ναίουσι ψυχαί, εἴδωλα καμόντων.

HOMERIC HYMN, *To the Earth*

Γαῖαν παμμήτειραν ἀείσομαι ἠϋθέμεθλον
πρεσβίστην, ἣ φέρβει ἐπὶ χθονὶ πάνθ' ὁπόσ' ἐστίν·
ἠμὲν ὅσα χθόνα δῖαν ἐπέρχεται ἠδ' ὅσα πόντον,
ἠδ' ὅσα πωτῶνται, τάδε φέρβεται ἐκ σέθεν ὄλβου.
ἐκ σέο δ' εὔπαιδές τε καὶ εὔκαρποι τελέθουσι
πότνια, σεῦ δ' ἔχεται δοῦναι βίον ἠδ' ἀφελέσθαι
θνητοῖς ἀνθρώποισιν· ὁ δ' ὄλβιος ὅν κε σὺ θυμῷ
πρόφρων τιμήσῃς· τῷ τ' ἄφθονα πάντα πάρεστι.
βρίθει μέν σφιν ἄρουρα φερέσβιος, ἠδὲ κατ' ἀγροὺς
κτήνεσιν εὐθηνεῖ, οἶκος δ' ἐμπίπλαται ἐσθλῶν·
αὐτοὶ δ' εὐνομίῃσι πόλιν κάτα καλλιγύναικα
κοιρανέουσ', ὄλβος δὲ πολὺς καὶ πλοῦτος ὀπηδεῖ·
παῖδες δ' εὐφροσύνῃ νεοθηλέϊ κυδιόωσι,
παρθενικαί τε χοροῖς φερεσανθέσιν εὔφρονι θυμῷ
παίζουσαι σκαίρουσι κατ' ἄνθεα μαλθακὰ ποίης,
οὕς κε σὺ τιμήσῃς σεμνὴ θεὰ ἄφθονε δαῖμον.
Χαῖρε θεῶν μήτηρ, ἄλοχ' Οὐρανοῦ ἀστερόεντος,
πρόφρων δ' ἀντ' ᾠδῆς βίοτον θυμήρε' ὄπαζε·
αὐτὰρ ἐγὼ καὶ σεῖο καὶ ἄλλης μνήσομ' ἀοιδῆς.

ANACREON, *Ode* XXXIII

Μεσονυκτίοις ποθ' ὥραις,
στρέφεται ὅτ' Ἄρκτος ἤδη
κατὰ χεῖρα τὴν Βοώτου,
μερόπων δὲ φῦλα πάντα
κέαται κόπῳ δαμέντα,

τότ' Ἔρως ἐπισταθείς μευ
θυρέων ἔκοπτ' ὀχῆας.
τίς, ἔφην, θύρας ἀράσσει;
κατά μευ σχίζεις ὀνείρους.
ὁ δ' Ἔρως, ἄνοιγε, φησίν·
βρέφος εἰμί, μὴ φόβησαι·
βρέχομαι δὲ κἀσέληνον
κατὰ νύκτα πεπλάνημαι.
ἐλέησα ταῦτ' ἀκούσας,
ἀνὰ δ' εὐθὺ λύχνον ἅψας
ἀνέῳξα, καὶ βρέφος μέν
ἐσορῶ φέροντα τόξον
πτέρυγάς τε καὶ φαρέτρην.
παρὰ δ' ἱστίην καθῖσα,
παλάμαις τε χεῖρας αὐτοῦ
ἀνέθαλπον, ἐκ δὲ χαίτης
ἀπέθλιβον ὑγρὸν ὕδωρ.
ὁ δ', ἐπεὶ κρύος μεθῆκεν,
φέρε, φησί, πειράσωμεν
τόδε τόξον, εἴ τι μοι νῦν
βλάβεται βραχεῖσα νευρή.
τανύει δὲ καί με τύπτει
μέσον ἧπαρ, ὥσπερ οἶστρος·
ἀνὰ δ' ἄλλεται καχάζων,
ξένε δ', εἶπε, συγχάρηθι·
κέρας ἀβλαβὲς μέν ἐστιν,
σὺ δὲ καρδίην πονήσεις.

CATULLUS, *Ode* XXXI

Paene insularum, Sirmio, insularumque
ocelle, quascumque in liquentibus stagnis
marique vasto fert uterque Neptunus;
quam te libenter quamque laetus inviso,
vix mi ipse credens Thuniam atque Bithunos
liquisse campos et videre te in tuto.
o quid solutis est beatius curis?
cum mens onus reponit, ac peregrino

labore fessi venimus larem ad nostrum,
desideratoque acquiescimus lecto.
hoc est quod unum est pro laboribus tantis.
salve o venusta Sirmio atque hero gaude;
gaudete vosque o Lydiae lacus undae;
ridete quidquid est domi cachinnorum.

VIRGIL, *Aeneid* VI, 269–294

perque domos Ditis vacuas et inania regna:
quale per incertam lunam sub luce maligna
est iter in silvis, ubi caelum condidit umbra
Iuppiter, et rebus nox abstulit atra colorem.
vestibulum ante ipsum primis in faucibus Orci
Luctus et ultrices posuere cubilia Curae;
pallentesque habitant Morbi tristisque Senectus,
et Metus et malesuada Fames ac turpis Egestas,
terribiles visu formae, Letumque Labosque;
tum consanguineus Leti Sopor et mala mentis
Gaudia, mortiferumque adverso in limine Bellum,
ferreique Eumenidum thalami et Discordia demens
vipereum crinem vittis innexa cruentis.
  In medio ramos annosaque bracchia pandit
ulmus opaca, ingens, quam sedem Somnia vulgo
vana tenere ferunt, foliisque sub omnibus haerent.
multaque praeterea variarum monstra ferarum,
Centauri in foribus stabulant Scyllaeque biformes
et centumgeminus Briareus ac belua Lernae
horrendum stridens, flammisque armata Chimaera,
Gorgones Harpyiaeque et forma tricorporis umbrae.
corripit hic subita trepidus formidine ferrum
Aeneas strictamque aciem venientibus offert,
et ni docta comes tenuis sine corpore vitas
admoneat volitare cava sub imagine formae,
inruat et frustra ferro diverberet umbras.

VIRGIL, *Georgics* I, 311–34

Quid tempestates autumni et sidera dicam,
atque, ubi iam breviorque dies et mollior aestas,
quae vigilanda viris? vel cum ruit imbriferum ver,
spicea iam campis cum messis inhorruit et cum
frumenta in viridi stipula lactentia turgent?
saepe ego, cum flavis messorem induceret arvis
agricola et fragili iam stringeret hordea culmo,
omnia ventorum concurrere proelia vidi,
quae gravidam late segetem ab radicibus imis
sublimem expulsam eruerent; ita turbine nigro
ferret hiems culmumque levem stipulasque volantis.
saepe etiam immensum caelo venit agmen aquarum
et foedam glomerant tempestatem imbribus atris
collectae ex alto nubes; ruit arduus aether,
et pluvia ingenti sata laeta boumque labores
diluit; implentur fossae et cava flumina crescunt
cum sonitu fervetque fretis spirantibus aequor.
ipse pater media nimborum in nocte corusca
fulmina molitur dextra: quo maxima motu
terra tremit; fugere ferae et mortalia corda
per gentis humilis stravit pavor: ille flagranti
aut Athon aut Rhodopen aut alta Ceraunia telo
deicit; ingeminant Austri et densissimus imber:
nunc nemora ingenti vento, nunc litora plangunt.

HORACE, *Odes* I, v

Quis multa gracilis te puer in rosa
perfusus liquidis urget odoribus
   grato, Pyrrha, sub antro?
    cui flavam religas comam

simplex munditiis? heu quotiens fidem
mutatosque deos flebit et aspera
   nigris aequora ventis
    emirabitur insolens,

qui nunc te fruitur credulus aurea,
qui semper vacuam, semper amabilem
    sperat, nescius aurae
        fallacis. miseri, quibus

intemptata nites. me tabula sacer
votiva paries indicat uvida
    suspendisse potenti
        vestimenta maris deo.

HORACE, *Odes* I, ix

Vides ut alta stet nive candidum
Soracte, nec iam sustineant onus
    silvae laborantes, geluque
        flumina constiterint acuto.

dissolve frigus ligna super foco
large reponens atque benignius
    deprome quadrimum Sabina,
        o Thaliarche, merum diota:

permitte divis cetera, qui simul
stravere ventos aequore fervido
    deproeliantis, nec cupressi
        nec veteres agitantur orni.

quid sit futurum cras fuge quaerere et
quem Fors dierum cumque dabit lucro
    appone, nec dulcis amores
        sperne puer neque tu choreas,

donec virenti canities abest
morosa. nunc et campus et areae
    lenesque sub noctem susurri
        composita repetantur hora,

nunc et latentis proditor intimo
gratus puellae risus ab angulo
    pignusque dereptum lacertis
        aut digito male pertinaci.

HORACE, *Odes* IV, vii

Diffugere nives, redeunt iam gramina campis
  arboribusque comae;
mutat terra vices, et decrescentia ripas
  flumina praetereunt;
Gratia cum Nymphis geminisque sororibus audet
  ducere nuda choros.
immortalia ne speres, monet annus et almum
  quae rapit hora diem:
frigora mitescunt Zephyris, ver proterit aestas
  interitura simul
pomifer Autumnus fruges effuderit, et mox
  bruma recurrit iners.
damna tamen celeres reparant caelestia lunae:
  nos ubi decidimus
quo pater Aeneas, quo Tullus dives et Ancus,
  pulvis et umbra sumus.
quis scit an adiciant hodiernae crastina summae
  tempora di superi?
cuncta manus avidas fugient heredis, amico
  quae dederis animo.
cum semel occideris et de te splendida Minos
  fecerit arbitria,
non, Torquate, genus, non te facundia, non te
  restituet pietas;
infernis neque enim tenebris Diana pudicum
  liberat Hippolytum,
nec Lethaea valet Theseus abrumpere caro
  vincula Perithoo.

DANTE, *Paradiso*, Canto XXXIII, 97–145

Così la mente mia, tutta sospesa,
  mirava fissa, immobile e attenta,
  e sempre di mirar faciesi accesa.
A quella luce cotal si diventa,
  che volgersi da lei per altro aspetto
  è impossibil che mai si consenta;

però che il ben, ch' è del volere obietto,
    tutto s' accoglie in lei; e fuor di quella
    è defettivo ciò ch' è lì perfetto.
Omai sarà più corta mia favella,
    pur a quel ch' io ricordo, che d' un fante
    che bagni ancor la lingua a la mammella.
Non perchè più ch' un semplice sembiante
    fosse nel vivo lume ch' io mirava,
    che tal è sempre qual s' era davante;
ma per la vista che s' avvalorava
    in me guardando, una sola parvenza,
    mutandom' io, a me si travagliava.
Ne la profonda e chiara sussistenza
    de l' alto lume parvermi tre giri
    di tre colori e d' una contenenza;
e l' un da l' altro come iri da iri
    parea reflesso, e 'l terzo parea foco
    che quinci e quindi igualmente si spiri.
Oh quanto è corto il dire e come fioco
    al mio concetto! e questo, a quel ch' i' vidi,
    è tanto, che non basta a dicer 'poco'.
O luce etterna che sola in te sidi,
    sola t' intendi, e da te intelletta
    e intendente te ami e arridi!
Quella circulazion che sì concetta
    pareva in te come lume reflesso,
    da li occhi miei alquanto circunspetta,
dentro da sè, del suo colore stesso,
    mi parve pinta de la nostra effige;
    per che 'l mio viso in lei tutto era messo.
Qual è 'l geometra che tutto s' affige
    per misurar lo cerchio, e non ritrova,
    pensando, quel principio ond' elli indige,
tal era io a quella vista nova:
    veder volea come si convenne
    l' imago al cerchio e come vi s' indova;
ma non eran da ciò le proprie penne:
    se non che la mia mente fu percossa
    da un fulgore in che sua voglia venne.

A l' alta fantasia qui mancò possa;
  ma già volgeva il mio disio e il velle,
  sì come rota ch' igualmente è mossa,
l' amor che move il sole e l' altre stelle.

CHAUCER, *The Nonne Preestes Tale*, 1–16

A povre widwe, somdel stape in age,
Was whylom dwelling in a narwe cotage,
Bisyde a grove, stonding in a dale.
This widwe, of which I telle yow my tale,
Sin thilke day that she was last a wyf,
In pacience hadde a ful simple lyf,
For litel was hir catel and hir rente;
By housbondrye, of such as God hir sente,
She fond hir-self, and eek hir doghtren two.
Three large sowes hadde she, and namo,
Three kine, and eek a sheep that highte Malle,
Ful sooty was hir bour, and eek hir halle,
In which she ate ful many a sclendre meel.
Of poynant sauce hir needed never a deel.
No deyntee morsel passed thurgh hir throte;
Hir dyete was accordant to hir cote.

NOTES ON THE MANUSCRIPT
POEMS OF SECTION I

[In preparing these notes I am greatly indebted to *English Poetical Autographs*, by Desmond Flower and A. N. L. Munby.   A.F.S.]

WILLIAM SHAKESPEARE. The play, *Sir Thomas More*, written, presumably, by Anthony Munday, has some passages which such eminent Shakespearean scholars as J. Dover Wilson, A. W. Pollard, W. W. Greg, and R. W. Chapman maintain to be not only by Shakespeare but in his autograph. One of these passages is reproduced here. (See *Shakespeare's Hand in the Play of Sir Thomas More*, Cambridge, 1923.)

GEORGE HERBERT. *Perfection*, composed by Herbert, was written down by another hand and corrected by the poet. The last verse, replacing the one deleted, is entirely in Herbert's autograph. This well-known poem was first published in *The Temple*, 1633.

JOHN MILTON. The poet writes of *Lycidas*, 'In this Monody the Author bewails a learned Friend, unfortunately drown'd in his passage from Chester on the Irish Seas, 1637.' This reproduction is of part of an early draft of the poem, written at Horton in November 1637, and published in the following year.

THOMAS GRAY. *The Elegy* was begun in 1742, soon after the death of Gray's friend, Richard West, and the poet continued to work upon the poem 'at irregular intervals during the next eight years'. The poem was first published in 1751 by Robert Dodsley, advised by Horace Walpole. This draft is in the Memorial Buildings at Eton College.

WILLIAM COWPER. Cowper wrote *The Halibut* in a letter dated 25 April 1784 to his friend Mary Unwin. It was not published till 1824, when Cowper's letters were first edited.

GEORGE CRABBE. *Jane Adair*, reproduced from one of Crabbe's autograph notebooks, is part of a longer poem entitled *Tracy*. Composed early in 1813, it was not published till 1907.

WILLIAM BLAKE. These first versions of *The Tyger* are written on two facing pages of the most famous of Blake's notebooks, known as the

Rossetti MS. The poem appeared in *Songs of Experience*, which Blake engraved and published himself in 1794.

WILLIAM WORDSWORTH. The basis of the manuscript of *The Waggoner* is a careful transcript made by Sara Hutchinson in 1806 from the rough drafts of the poems. Upon this transcript Wordsworth laboured during a period of thirteen years, as he himself records. The passage reproduced here has been worked over, cancelled and revised in Wordsworth's hand.

S. T. COLERIDGE. *Lewti* was first published in the *Morning Post*, 13 April 1798. Though intended for inclusion in the *Lyrical Ballads*, it was withdrawn at the last moment. It was included in the *Annual Anthology*, 1800, and *Sibylline Leaves* in 1817.

LORD BYRON. *Oh! Snatch'd away in Beauty's Bloom* was written at the request of Byron's friend the Hon. Douglas Kinnaird for a *Selection of Hebrew Melodies*, and was published, with the music by the composer Isaac Nathan, in April 1815.

P. B. SHELLEY. Among Shelley's manuscript fragments occur two undated translations; one, of a part of Bion's *Lament for Adonis*, is reproduced here; the other is a part of Moschus' *Elegy on the Death of Bion*. These were first published by H. Buxton Forman in 1876.

JOHN KEATS. This is a reproduction of the first draft of the *Ode to a Nightingale* made by the poet on 30 April 1819. His friend Charles Brown said that Keats wrote it under the plum-tree in the garden at Wentworth Place, Hampstead. The poem was published in the July number of *Annals of the Fine Arts* for 1819, and reprinted in *Lamia and other Poems*, 1820.

T. L. BEDDOES. The poet sent a copy of *Dream Pedlary* to his friend Kelsall in a letter dated 19 July 1830. The poem is reproduced here from the MS. of an early version in the British Museum.

LORD TENNYSON. *Milton: Alcaics*, an experiment in quantity, was first printed in *The Cornhill Magazine*, December 1863. It was reprinted in *Idylls of the Hearth*, 1864, subsequently known as *Enoch Arden and other Poems*.

ROBERT BROWNING. This passage from *The Ring and the Book* is reproduced from the MS. copy of the poem in the British Museum on which Browning worked 'four full years unintermittingly' from 1864. The poem was published in four volumes in the winter of 1868–69.

E. B. BROWNING. *The Runaway Slave at Pilgrim's Point* was written at Pisa in the autumn of 1847, and sent to America. It was published in Boston, in *The Liberty Bell*, in 1848, and separately in England in 1849.

D. G. ROSSETTI. This is a reproduction of the first draft of *Love's Compass* published in *Poems*, 1870. It was one of the group of sonnets which later formed part of *The House of Life*.

CHRISTINA ROSSETTI. *Sleeping at Last* was written about 1893. It was published in 1896 in a posthumous volume entitled *New Poems* edited by the poet's brother W. M. Rossetti.

A. C. SWINBURNE. This is a reproduction of part of the first draft of *Rococo* in the large collection of Swinburne's MS. poems in the British Museum. The poem was first published in *Poems and Ballads*, 1866.

G. M. HOPKINS. *Starlight Night* was written on 24 February 1877. Robert Bridges kept a MS. book in which he pasted Hopkins' poems, in the author's handwriting, as he received them. This is a reproduction of the draft in the MS. book now in the Bodleian Library. The poem was first published in Miles' *Poets and Poetry of the Century*, 1897.

EDWARD THOMAS. This first draft of *Adlestrop*, in the thin exercise book in the British Museum containing many of Thomas's manuscript poems, was written in 1916 and published in the following year.

RUPERT BROOKE. This is a reproduction of the first of several drafts of *The Soldier*. This sonnet first appeared in *New Numbers*, 1914. It was reprinted in *1914 and Other Poems* in the year 1915. The MSS. are in the Library of King's College, Cambridge.

WILFRED OWEN. The amendments to *Anthem for Dead Youth* were made in pencil by Siegfried Sassoon when, at Craiglockhart, near Edinburgh, in September 1917, Wilfred Owen showed him the first draft of the sonnet which is reproduced here. The title was changed later to *Anthem for Doomed Youth*.

ISAAC ROSENBERG. The first draft of *Moses*, part of which is reproduced here, was written in 1916 on rough scraps of paper. Rosenberg's only publications during his life were three pamphlets: *Night and Day*, *Youth*, and *Moses, A Play*, all published at his own expense.

BOOK LIST

The following books are suggested for further study:

F. W. BATESON, *English Poetry: A Critical Introduction* (Longmans).

C. M. BOWRA, *The Heritage of Symbolism* (Macmillan).

——, *The Creative Experiment* (Macmillan).

NORMAN CALLAN, *Poetry in Practice* (Lindsay Drummond).

T. S. ELIOT, *Selected Essays* (Faber).

——, *The Use of Poetry and the Use of Criticism* (Faber).

——, *The Music of Poetry* (Glasgow University Publications).

W. EMPSON, *Seven Types of Ambiguity* (Chatto and Windus).

A. H. GARDINER, *The Theory of Speech and Language* (Oxford University Press).

ROBERT GRAVES, *On English Poetry* (Heinemann).

A. E. HOUSMAN, *The Name and Nature of Poetry* (Cambridge University Press).

W. P. KER, *Collected Essays* (Macmillan).

——, *Epic and Romance* (Macmillan).

——, *Form and Style in Poetry* (Macmillan).

F. R. LEAVIS, *New Bearings in English Poetry* (Chatto and Windus).

——, *Revaluation* (Chatto and Windus).

F. R. LEAVIS (ed.), *Determinations* (Chatto and Windus).

C. DAY LEWIS, *A Hope for Poetry* (Blackwell).

——, *The Poetic Image* (Cape).

C. S. LEWIS, *Rehabilitations* (Oxford University Press).

F. L. LUCAS, *The Decline and Fall of the Romantic Ideal* (Cambridge University Press).

P. H. B. LYON, *The Discovery of Poetry* (Arnold).

LOUIS MACNEICE, *Modern Poetry* (Oxford University Press).

JOHN PRESS, *The Fire and the Fountain* (Oxford University Press).

HERBERT READ, *Form in Modern Poetry* (Sheed and Ward).

——, *Phases of English Poetry* (Hogarth Press).

I. A. RICHARDS, *Principles of Literary Criticism* (Kegan Paul).

——, *Practical Criticism* (Kegan Paul).

——, *Science and Poetry* (Kegan Paul).

M. R. RIDLEY, *Poetry and the Ordinary Reader* (Bell).

BOOK LIST

STEPHEN SPENDER, *The Destructive Element* (Cape).

——, *World within World* (Hamish Hamilton).

——, *The Making of a Poem* (Hamish Hamilton).

MARTIN TURNELL, *Poetry and Crisis* (Sands).

EDMUND WILSON, *Axel's Castle* (Scribner's).

——, *The Wound and the Bow* (W. H. Allen).